First Across the Continent

Other Books by Barry Gough

The Royal Navy and the Northwest Coast of North America
(Vancouver, 1971)
To the Pacific and Arctic with Beechey (ed.) (Cambridge, 1973)
Canada (Englewood Cliffs, N.J., 1975)
Distant Dominion (Vancouver, 1980)
Gunboat Frontier (Vancouver, 1984)
Journal of Alexander Henry the Younger (ed.) (Toronto, 1988,
1992)
The Falkland Islands/Malvinas (London, 1992)
The Northwest Coast (Vancouver, 1992)

First Across the Continent

SIR ALEXANDER MACKENZIE

By Barry Gough

M&S

Published in the United States by the University of Oklahoma Press as Volume 14 in The Oklahoma Western Biographies (Richard W. Etulain, General Editor).

Although the series volumes carry no footnotes, they are prepared by leading scholars, are soundly researched, and include a brief listing of sources used. Each volume is a lively synthesis based on a thorough examination of pertinent primary and secondary sources.

Published simultaneously in Canada by McClelland & Stewart Inc.

Canadian Cataloguing in Publication Data

Gough, Barry M., 1938–
    First across the continent : Sir Alexander Mackenzie

Includes bibliographical references and index.
ISBN 0-7710-3406-7

1. Mackenzie, Alexander, Sir, 1764–1820.   2. Northwest, Canadian—Discovery and exploration.   3. Fur trade—Canada—History.   4. Indians of North America—Canada—History.   5. Explorers—Canada—Biography.   6. Fur traders—Canada—Biography.   I. Title.

FC3212.1.M46G68   1997   971.2'01'092   C97-930884-4
F1060.7.M1783G68   1997

Printed and bound in the United States of America

McClelland & Stewart, Inc.
The Canadian Publishers
481 University Avenue
Toronto, Ontario
M5G 2E9

1 2 3 4 5   01 00 99 98 97

For W. Kaye Lamb and John S. Galbraith

Contents

Illustrations

PHOTOGRAPHS

MAPS

Editor's Preface

In this lively, smoothly written biography, Barry Gough provides a well-organized and engrossing account of Alexander Mackenzie, the notable Canadian explorer. The early chapters of Gough's biography illuminate Mackenzie's Scottish background, his beginnings in the New World, and his initial efforts in the North American fur trade. But the major focus of *First Across the Continent: Sir Alexander Mackenzie* is Mackenzie's memorable trip in 1789 down the river that now bears his name and his arduous journey to the Pacific in 1793. Mackenzie's explorations, which predate the Lewis and Clark expedition, made many important geographical discoveries and opened Canada to its northern destiny. In a final section, the author discusses Mackenzie's efforts to shape commercial and governmental policies in the North American West before his death in 1820.

In readable fashion, Gough supplies a multifaceted portrait of an engaging and powerful character. Here are clear evidences of Mackenzie's drive, his overpowering ambition, and his relentless desire to push back the shadowy curtain covering much of western Canada. A man of immense energy and courage, Mackenzie drove himself and his men mercilessly; yet as a tireless leader, he demanded as much of himself as of his underlings.

To his credit, Gough also deals with the darker side of Mackenzie's life. While independent, forceful, and indefatigable, Mackenzie was likewise driven by his "bulldog persistence," his need for attention, and his huge ego. In one apt phrase, the author discerns Mackenzie's motivations: if he "could not have it to his advantage, he would not have it at all." As Gough shows, on several occasions Mackenzie resorted to questionable actions to achieve his goals; in these situations, he seemed not to worry if his deeds infringed on the rights of others.

Gough also places Mackenzie clearly within his turbulent times. As the herald of a new age, Mackenzie opened the door for flurries of planning and acting in the realms of commerce, international politics, and scientific study. Most of all, Gough's Mackenzie rightfully takes his place among the elite of New World explorers and empire builders.

In short, Barry Gough's revealing study of Sir Alexander Mackenzie provides an illuminating biography of an important western figure and situates that life story within the wider historical currents of its time.

RICHARD W. ETULAIN
GENERAL EDITOR
THE OKLAHOMA WESTERN BIOGRAPHIES

University of New Mexico

Preface

IN brief compass this book is a record of Mackenzie's life from birth to death. It also draws his life into the history of the North American, principally Canadian, fur trade, with all its international affiliations. Moreover, this book links Mackenzie's life to British imperial commercial regulation and thus, by definition, to Anglo-American rivalry. Mackenzie ranks among the central figures in the fur trade of the late eighteenth and early nineteenth centuries. In the era before 1821 the Hudson's Bay Company, based in London, England, dominated the commerce of northernmost North America in furs. In this period the Montreal-centered trade witnessed a titanic struggle for control and monopoly in which Mackenzie played an important role.

This book rests heavily on Mackenzie's famous work, published in 1801 under the title of *Voyages from Montreal on the River St. Laurence through the Continent of North America to the Frozen and Pacific Oceans in the Years 1789 and 1793 with a Preliminary Account of the Rise, Progress, and Present State of the Fur Trade of That Country Illustrated with Maps*. His book was based on his worked-up journals, kept during his travels. Except where otherwise indicated, all quotations from his *Voyages from Montreal* are taken from the original edition or as reproduced by the Hakluyt Society in a volume prepared by W. Kaye Lamb in 1970. Literary experts and critics, among them two distinguished scholars, Roy Daniells and Ian MacLaren, have demonstrated the closeness of Mackenzie's 1789 journal to the final printed version. On their authority we can be assured that Mackenzie was an extraordinarily competent writer, perhaps the best of those in the fur trade. We can also be persuaded that his work was little tampered with, and then only cosmetically, before reaching print. *Voyages from Montreal* is a remarkable work, containing as it does a history of the Canadian fur trade now generally attributed to Mackenzie's cousin Roderick. Mackenzie's 1789 narrative, now in the Department of Manuscripts of the British Library in London, has been published as *Exploring the Northwest Territory* (University of Oklahoma Press, 1966), edited by T. H. Mc-Donald. In the pages that follow, this text is cited as "Journal."

The documentary sources upon which this book is based are not only extensive but also readily available. This book, like others in the same series, does not contain footnotes. Where I have quoted directly from sources, I have made specific internal documentation so that the inquisitive reader wishing to follow up such matters may readily find the sources used. In the commentary on sources at the end of this book, readers will find a complete guide to the materials, both primary and secondary, on which this book is based.

In writing this book, it has been my plan to take the reader along with Alexander Mackenzie on his travels and voyages, and to present, through a strong narrative line, the problems faced by the trading explorer. I employ direct quotations at certain places to give a vivid sense of how Mackenzie saw the circumstances and how he faced various difficulties. I have searched for new scraps of information that would allow a greater understanding of the inner man and would permit the writing of an interior biography. In the end, I have been obliged to be content with reinterpreting extant sources—which are considerable—and casting new light wherever possible on the motivations and perplexities of a young Scot who traversed more territory in his youth than many others ever dreamed of and who made a fortune in a wilderness that he came in the end to regret because of its isolation from his preferred social circles. The research and writing of this book have given good reason for visiting or revisiting certain locations in Canada and Scotland that feature in the text. In Scotland my travels took me to Stornoway on the Isle of Lewis and to Avoch on the Black Isle—respectively, Mackenzie's birthplace and final resting place. Like Samuel Johnson, who toured the Western Islands with James Boswell in 1773, the last year that Alexander Mackenzie resided at home before his departure for America, I expected to find a wilder, earlier state of things than I actually encountered. It would have been wonderful to recapture a vision of the antiquated life of legend and the more primitive character of Highland life, but today the inhabitants of these locales, like those residing near the mouth of the Mackenzie River or at Bella Coola, are preoccupied with workaday life. Yet my challenge as biographer remains—to recreate the past and make sense of it through the eyes of the subject—and visions of place and recreations of locations can bring to the reader a sense of how things might have been. In an attempt to portray Alexander Mackenzie against the tumultuous social conditions of the Scotland from which he emigrated, I have delved into relevant aspects of this branch of history. In this way I have sought to incorporate the Mackenzie progression into the larger themes of those British and Highland emigration annals that continue to receive prominent attention at the hands of Bernard Bailyn, Jack Bumstead, John Prebble, David Craig, John Hunter, and others.

In Canada I have explored Mackenzie's pathways as much as time and money would allow, believing—as Francis Parkman instructed—that a historian should know the lay of the land. I have traveled from Montreal to the Pacific, voyaged the Great Lakes, trudged across the Grand Portage, forded the Peace River, and stood on the shores of the Backwater, Fraser, Athabasca, and other rivers of Mackenzie's experience, including "River Disappointment" itself. From the air I have seen much of the mountainous terrain that stood between Mackenzie and easy success. It was not possible for me to follow each and every mile of his route. But I have sat at my desk for many an hour wondering how it was possible two centuries ago to make two gigantic thrusts into the unknown wilderness—one north, the other west—and to live to tell such a splendid tale. As a historian I can recreate this experience for the reader and be an intermediary between present and past, but I do so with a sense of regret that I am unable to interview Alexander Mackenzie in person. I have had to be content with reading his narrative and all surviving textual records of his challenges and his achievements. And in contrast to critics who carp that Mackenzie was simply on a guided tour, I stand in awe of his success.

An extensive bibliographical search with the assistance of the National Archives of Canada, Reference Division, and the Map Library of the National Archives of Canada has made available copies of Mackenzie's maps. In the British Library Department of Manuscripts I consulted the fair copy of Mackenzie's 1789 journal and the Haldimand Papers. In the Map Library of the same institution I uncovered the emendations by Joseph Colen to the 1796 edition of Aaron Arrowsmith's chart of new discoveries, which show Mackenzie's achievements as measured, so to speak, by the cartographic world of that time. A grant from Wilfrid Laurier University allowed me to press on with my research and to bring this project to an earlier completion than would otherwise have been possible. I benefited from the holdings of the University of Cambridge Library, the Scott Polar Research Institute, and the Kitchener Public Library.

I wish to acknowledge the help of many persons who assisted in this work. I thank W. Kaye Lamb for his excellent editorial work and for his assistance over many years.

Roy Daniells, my neighbor in Victoria and my professor in Vancouver, early lauded interplays of land and sea in Canadian history, and with avuncular interest understood my purpose in drawing together strands of history to make a single cloth.

Thomas Vaughan and the Oregon Historical Society willingly embraced the addition of a Canadian dimension to the organization's western exploration series, and this allowed me to chart the aspects of nascent Canadian trade to Asia.

Doug MacDonald of the Canadian Broadcasting Corporation shared his lively interest in Mackenzie's Scottish years, and opened many new doors for me.

In Stornoway Frank Thompson and Murdoch MacLeod provided help, and in Avoch retired Seaforth Highlander Gregor Macintosh and his wife Annie shared their enthusiasm for the fur-trading explorer. To be with them and their associates Robert Legget of Ottawa, Major Allan Cameron, the county convenor of Ross and Cromarty Council, and distinguished guests at Mackenzie's burial place to unveil a memorial tablet on the occasion of the bicentenary of Mackenzie's arrival on Pacific shores is a memory not soon to be forgotten.

The Dowager Countess of Cromarty, whose late husband was historian of the clan, provided insights into Scottish life in the eighteenth and nineteenth centuries.

James Shaw Grant shared his knowledge of Stornoway history.

Clive Holland reviewed the text and unearthed Mackenzie's 1819 advice to John Franklin, which is reprinted as appendix 2 of this book through courtesy of the Scott Polar Research Institute.

Ian MacLaren encouraged the project, and came to my rescue on several occasions.

The Alexander Mackenzie Voyageur Route Association, especially its founder John Woodworth, provided specifics about Mackenzie's Pacific expedition; members of this society have kept alive Mackenzie's memory in the face of all sorts of indifference.

In Peace River, Alberta, members of the Sir Alexander Mackenzie Historical Society counseled me on Mackenzie's travels in that area and conducted me to the site of his riverside winter haven.

I thank Arlene Staicesku for hospitality and the Peace River Centennial Museum and Archives for copies of documents relating to the history of Fort Fork.

Caron Riley of Peace River verified data on Mackenzie's relations with a native woman, the Catt, at Fort Chipewyan.

Oliver Glanfield of the Fort Chipewyan Historical Society gave details on Chipewyan language.

Wilma Schreder and the Dene Cultural Institute provided information and assistance.

Bill Lawson of Northton, Outer Hebrides, checked genealogical data.

Those avid students of Canadian fur trade history in Glengarry County, Ontario, Ian Bowering, David Anderson, and Hugh MacMillan, have provided fresh insights.

Rob Caldwell and Fred Gaskin, likewise canoe enthusiasts, saved me from navigational hazards on the Mackenzie.

Andrew Stubbs, Bruce Hodgins, Chris Hagerman, and Michael Bravo listened to my musings and broadened my horizons.

The late Dr. Helen Wallis of the British Library helped with maps.

Archivists and librarians of many repositories, especially

the Stornoway Public Library, the British Library, the National Archives of Canada, the Hudson's Bay Archives in Winnipeg (copies of which are in the Public Record Office in London), and the British Columbia Archives and Records Service, have provided professional assistance when called upon.

R. L. Greaves drew the maps.

I particularly thank Edward Dahl of Ottawa for his advice on maps.

Others who provided help and encouragement or read sections of the text were Glyndwr Williams, John Naish, H. B. Carter, Beau Riffenburgh, John Woodworth, Edrie Holloway, Robert Headland, Melinda Gough, William Swagerty, A. M. (Sandy) Robinson, Kent Sedgwick, Peter Melnycky, and B. Guild Gillespie.

My editors Richard Etulain and John Drayton, and associates, encouraged this project and saw it through the publication process. Lys Ann Shore copyedited the manuscript.

Anonymous readers provided insightful commentary that assisted in shaping the narrative and analysis.

To all these, and to others whom I may have inadvertently missed, I express my thanks. I alone am responsible for the opinions stated herein.

BARRY GOUGH

Waterloo, Ontario

First Across the Continent

The discovery of a passage by sea, North-East or North-West from the Atlantic to the Pacific Ocean, has for many years excited the attention of governments, and encouraged the enterprising spirit of individuals. The non-existence, however, of any such practical passage being at length determined, the practicability of a passage through the continents of Asia and America becomes an object of consideration. The Russians, who first discovered that, along the coasts of Asia no useful or regular navigation existed, opened an interior communication by rivers, & through that long and wide-extended continent, to the strait that separates Asia from America, over which they passed to the adjacent islands and continent of the latter. Our situation, at length, is in some degree similar to theirs; the non-existence of a practicable passage by sea, and the existence of one through the continent, are clearly proved; and it requires only the countenance and support of the British Government, to increase in a very ample proportion this national advantage, and secure the trade of that country to its subjects.

Experience, however, has proved, that this trade, from its very nature cannot be carried on by individuals. A very large capital, or credit, or indeed both, is necessary, and consequently an association of men of wealth to direct, with men of enterprise to act, in one common interest, must be formed on such principles, as that in due time the latter may succeed the former, in continual and progressive succession. Such was the equitable and successful mode adopted by the Merchants from Canada.

ALEXANDER MACKENZIE,
Voyages from Montreal *(1801)*

Introduction

SIR Alexander Mackenzie ranks as one of the most remarkable persons of North American wilderness history and, indeed, as one of the greatest travelers of all time. We would know more about him if his personal papers and diaries had not gone up in smoke in the fire that ruined his Scottish retirement house. Even so, a great deal of material exists upon which to base an account of his life. Various biographers have gone before me in attempting to reconstitute the life of this remarkable man. All, however, have failed to appreciate one fundamental fact—that his life in the wilderness was dedicated to one grand purpose, the making of money. This biography portrays a traveler in pursuit of profit. Mackenzie's imperial motives—to expand the horizons of British trade and the British empire—were underscored by geographical needs, philosophical precepts, and scientific requirements of his age.

Mackenzie's epic voyage to the mouth of the great northern river that now bears his name would have been enough to give him an unchallenged place in the history of frontier exploration. Yet he went well beyond this momentous achievement. His celebrated and even more arduous overland expedition a few years later from Lake Athabasca in northwestern Canada to Pacific saltwater near Dean Channel in what is now British Columbia marked him out as "the first [European] man west," the pioneer of transcontinental exploration north of the Rio Grande. Twelve years before

Lewis and Clark blazed their remarkable trail across America, Mackenzie painted his name on a rock by the Pacific shore, thereby announcing his arrival on the Northwest Coast and his transcontinental journey.

Native claims to historical priority and precedence, though undeniably significant, do not diminish what we owe to Mackenzie as the first to open this particular North American expanse to the eyes of the whole world. His surveys of the vast Canadian Northwest are graphic testaments to the role played by fur traders in unlocking, for the wider world, the secrets of half a continent. His dealings with Canadian fur traders and voyageurs speak volumes about the business in pelts of the late eighteenth century. His contact with native peoples, at that time little known to and less well understood by Europeans, remained central to every step of his progress. Dependent on native guides and labor for easing his way through tortuous terrain and unknown wilderness, Mackenzie was at the mercy of Indian military capability. He was on sufferance as he passed through lands controlled by powerful and sometimes suspicious, even hostile, native tribes. His discoveries were bittersweet, for they did not show an easy-to-travel route, the river of the West so long promised by armchair geographers. Rather, his explorations revealed the true nature of the North and the transmountain West: a hazardous, difficult, and demanding terrain coursed by winding rivers and dominated by difficult natives.

The promise of the Canadian Northwest was revealed by this young Scot. He pursued Canada's commercial possibilities with energy and dedication coupled with clear-thinking realism and pragmatism. Fighting indifference to commercial prospects within the corporation, the North West Company, and struggling against vested interests in the fur trade of the British Empire, dominated by the Hudson's Bay Company, Mackenzie lobbied colonial governors in Canada and imperial statesmen in London to embrace his dream for an empire of trade and commerce in the North Pacific. In this he was unsuccessful. Even so, his designs were eventually taken up by the Nor'Westers, by rival Bay traders, and by the British government. Indeed, by the time of his death, this pathfinder of Canadian and North American commerce knew that despite unending difficulties, he had lived to participate in a vast scheme of trade that linked Montreal with the Columbia River and the Atlantic world with the markets of China. This northern Sinbad left a legacy that is remarkable for its connections among rival fur companies, its links with the United States and with Russia, and its shaping of a separate destiny for Canada in western North America.

At least one previous biographer has spoken of Mackenzie's failures. Still others have given him less than his due as a businessman. However, like other Nor'Westers, Mackenzie lived within the parameters of the trading relationships of the day. He was, besides, obliged to conform to the majority trading interests of the concern. Mackenzie stood determined to convince others of the need for exploration and initiative—what corporations of our time would call research and development. To push his own schemes, he often engaged in internal corporate wars. On one occasion he went so far as to quit the corporation and set up his own renegade company, making it a profitable concern until such time as rival, more conservative or reactionary, forces were swept aside.

In Mackenzie's business activities are to be found the secrets to his motivations, to his aspirations for the British Empire in northern latitudes and on northern seas, and to his future hopes. He carefully charted a course through a minefield of complications and obstacles. The wilderness offered him a place for profitable speculation, and he mastered it to fulfill his private aims of personal wealth. Many other traders tried the same thing and failed. To Mackenzie alone can be credited two gigantic, successful wilderness sorties—the first to the North, the second to the West— that earned him a place in history.

Mackenzie's relationships with other individuals provide us with a window on eighteenth-century North America. Traders and investors whom he encountered show him to have been at or near the hub of commercial relationships, never far from the center of gravity of the St. Lawrence empire. He borrowed liberally from the enigmatic Peter Pond, who had opened the rich Athabasca country to the fur trade based in Grand Portage and the St. Lawrence. Mackenzie quarreled mightily with Simon McTavish, known as "the Marquis" or "the Premier," who dominated the North West Company until his death. Mackenzie's western explorations sparked President Thomas Jefferson's designs for an official exploration by the U.S. Corps of Discovery headed by Meriwether Lewis and William Clark. Mackenzie's trading activities also alarmed the directors and field managers of the rival Hudson's Bay Company, who sought to counter his initiatives. His cross-border trading to eager entrepreneurs in Philadelphia and New York, as a means of countering British mercantile regulation, opened the first Canada-to-China trade. By this subterfuge, Mackenzie enabled business to be transacted between the Western world and the East at a time when restrictive regulation was the order of the day and free trade unheard of.

Known at the British court, this upwardly mobile Scot of ordinary birth was made a knight bachelor for his famous book describing his remarkable travels. He sat for a portrait by the celebrated Sir Thomas Lawrence. His is an international story linking a remarkable collection of individuals in the British Isles, Canada, the United States, and continental Europe. His eventual retirement to his native Scotland, where he became a laird, completed the generous cycle of his experiences. Mackenzie understood the business climate of his times and shaped it largely according to his needs. That he was not entirely successful is a tribute to the ancient power of vested interests and to the prevailing movement toward monopoly, a marked feature of the Canadian fur trade. In his latter years he faced increasing competition from John Jacob Astor, whose business was based in New York. As the Canadian-American boundary was being established and regulated, Mackenzie fought against the Americanization of the trade on the southern frontier of Canada's commercial realm in furs. In latter years, too, Mackenzie fought against Earl Selkirk and the colonization of the Red and Assiniboine river forks. The trap line was pitted against the plough, and in the end it was settlement that gained the day. Mackenzie championed the North West Company's last defense against the settlers and against the Hudson's Bay Company, which had become party to the agrarian schemes of Selkirk. Mackenzie marks the final chapter of an old order.

.

CHAPTER I

Lords of Lakes and Forests

THE snug port of Stornoway in the rocky, sea-girt Isle of Lewis, one of Scotland's Western Isles or Outer Hebrides, lies in the same latitude as Fort Chipewyan, Lake Athabasca, in northwestern Canadaa. These two northern locations, though on opposite sides of the Atlantic Ocean, were brought into historical conjunction by the life of Sir Alexander Mackenzie.

Stornoway and Lewis were places of legend where the Mackenzies of Seaforth flourished in times past. There Alexander was born in the year 1762, and not in 1763 or 1764 as has been previously speculated, for his emigrant record of 1774 gives his age as twelve. His place of birth was no crofter's cottage or terrace house but a handsome west-facing, slate-roofed house at the corner of Francis and Kenneth Streets, where Martin's Memorial Church now stands. Today a bronze inscription tells the wayfarer that Mackenzie, "the first white man to follow the Mackenzie River to the Arctic Ocean," was also "the first to cross the Continent of North America north of Mexico."

Mackenzie hailed from a celebrated region that gave to Canada many Celtic gifts and tender remembrances—as the early Canadian poet, John Galt, so hauntingly testified:

From the lone shieling of the misty island
Mountains divide us, and the waste of seas—
Yet still the blood is strong, the heart is Highland,

And we in dreams behold the Hebrides!
Fair these broad meads, these hoary woods are grand;
But we are exiles from our fathers' land.

As an infant, Alexander relocated with his family two miles
eastward from Stornoway to a flatland agricultural holding
at a place called Melbost. Nowadays visitors can see nothing
of the farm where Mackenzie spent his childhood. Yet there
is no denying the maritime nature of the place, for nearby
the rocky shoreline leads to the sea. And the sea in turn
flows to the four corners of the globe.

Over such waterways in the eighteenth century and afterward Scots were carried to new and often unexpected places
of opportunity. In Mackenzie's day they went outward from
the home islands in great numbers. Soldiers returning to
Scotland from campaigns in colonial America told of unbounded wealth and opportunity in the New World. Speculators advertised land for sale in America and sent ships to
the isles to take off would-be settlers and bond-servants.
Glowing accounts of the riches of America were published
throughout the Highlands. Wealthy and poor alike made
for New York, Philadelphia, and North Carolina.

During the first decade of Alexander's life in the Hebrides,
some twenty thousand Highlanders left their homes for the
other side of the Atlantic. General James Grant, a contemporary, said that people thought less of a journey to America
than they did of a trip to London. In the four years before
Alexander Mackenzie's departure, two thousand people
sailed from Lewis alone; in 1773 eight hundred sailed from
Stornoway, bound for North Carolina. Soldiers and others
at such public occasions, with pipes, drums, and fiddles to
rouse their spirits for the expedition overseas, launched this
grand emigration. At community parties the Scots did a
"Dance Called America" in which everything was in motion,

and moving outward from the center, much like what society was experiencing.

As to the emigrants, they sought a better life elsewhere. Nothing remained to keep them in Scotland. The main landlord of the island, the Laird Seaforth (or Lord Fortrose as he then was), became so alarmed by the size of this exodus that he sought to put a stop to it. Government put in place regulations to try to check emigration. However, the forces for quitting the islands and Highlands were compelling. Great distress had fallen on the land. A sense of despair had descended upon the common people. Inflation, heavy rains, indifferent or failed crops, and rising rents all spelled reasons for quitting hearth and home. Poverty and famine stalked the land. The collector of customs in Stornoway, following instructions, employed an agent to inquire into the reasons why people were leaving Stornoway. A double-barreled question was always put to the leader of the departing party: "On what account and for what purpose are you leaving the country?" The agent noted in his report the collective reply: "All emigrated in order to procure a living abroad as they were quite destitute for bread and hope."

All was then in crisis in Scottish life, and swift and surprising changes were coming to Scotland. Old relationships were being broken up; discontent and insecurity were widely felt. "We came thither too late to see what we expected, a people of peculiar appearance, and a system of antiquated life," bemoaned the celebrated traveler Dr. Samuel Johnson of his visit with James Boswell to the Hebrides in 1773. To this Johnson added with rare insight into the times: "The clans retain little now of their original character, their ferocity of temper is softened, their military ardour is extinguished, their dignity of independence is depressed, their contempt of government subdued, and their reverence for their chiefs abated. Of what they had before the late conquest of their country, there remain only their language and their poverty." This last observation was quite true, for Alexander Mackenzie's family was downwardly mobile, and rapidly so.

Mackenzie's family was not, however, in the distressed class, for family members were managers, soldiers, and entrepreneurs. Alexander's father had grown up in a tribal system, in which a native was by definition and tradition a man of war. But ancient customs of the Highlands and islands were being swept away swiftly as a result of the Jacobite risings. Before the military power of the chiefs collapsed at Culloden in 1746, clan chiefs had measured their rent power by the number of men they could muster for military purposes. Alexander Mackenzie's father and grandfather were "cadets" of the Mackenzie clan, holding importance and dignity second only in precedence to the chief, or laird. They were the gentlemen of the clan, and they held the land allotted them by the chief for a length of time called a tack; thus they were called tacksmen.

Alexander's father, Kenneth Mackenzie, was one such, and to him as to others were let sizable agricultural holdings, such as the holding at Melbost, according to their importance and nominal rent. After 1746, however, they were the first to suffer and lose their lands. They thought the lairds mercenary in their demands for rent money—something entirely new—for previously these men had been prepared to lay down their lives in combat for the clan chief. They felt grossly aggrieved for having been treated so injudiciously. As sons were born to the chief, so tacksmen were displaced, and accordingly the sons of those tacksmen might alarmingly soon become part of the common folk of the clan. This explains why Alexander's older brother Murdoch could not follow his father as a tacksman but instead trained as a surgeon. Younger sons normally were sent to join French or Spanish armies and were married off as soon as possible. Seldom if ever were they trained for business or other employments. Left to their good fortune and conduct abroad, they often enjoyed a brighter future than those obliged to stay at home in farming or commerce. Alexander, if he had stayed in Scotland, would have been destined for a declining status and might even have degenerated to the rank of commoner—a destitute one at that—unless some sudden acquisition of wealth could have supported him above his station.

Alexander Mackenzie entered this world of crisis as a member of a strong, well-placed family with identifiable roots in Kintail and a genealogy traced to a thirteenth-century chief named Kenneth. Throughout the course of the fifteenth century the clan had grown wealthy, and despite prolonged problems during civil war and religious strife the Mackenzies had risen to extensive influence in two parts of the kingdom: Lewis in the Western Isles and lands adjoining Moray Firth on the eastern flanks of Scotland. Both these heartlands featured in the explorer's life.

From scattered evidence we can paint a picture of Alexander Mackenzie's father, Kenneth Mackenzie of Stornoway. He appears as a tough-minded, heavy-handed soldier loyal to King George and willing to take up military obligations. He seems to have been commercially progressive, leaving the old ways of Scotland behind him. A powerful fellow, known locally by the nickname of Cork, Kenneth Mackenzie was grandson of Allan Mackenzie of Stornoway and son of Donald Mackenzie of Fairburn, near Dingwall in Ross and Cromarty. As his son Alexander did later, Kenneth Mackenzie kept up a connection between two parts of northern Scotland, the Western Isles and the Highlands. His great place of activity was Stornoway. He may have been the hard-driving factor, or manager, to the demanding Lord Fortrose, mentioned in Captain Barlow's report about Stornoway in 1753. Kenneth Mackenzie was an army officer and merchant and may also have been a well-fixed possessor of tacks. Certainly he was a chieftain, and thus one to whom those below looked up as their leader. He and his kind commanded the military expeditions, and this, not agriculture, was their main employment. Kenneth Mackenzie was sufficiently well situated in the community to serve as ensign in the Stornoway Company of Volunteers, who were called to arms in 1745 to hunt down the pretender to the throne, Prince Charles Edward Stuart. Bonnie Prince Charlie, it seems, sought to acquire a boat in Stornoway so that he could be safely conveyed to France; in the event, however, the alarms and excursions resulted in no action except for the Stornoway volunteers being aroused. We may surmise that Kenneth played a major role in this affair.

Alexander's mother, Isabella Maciver, similarly came from one of Stornoway's leading families, one with progressive mercantile pursuits in America. She married Kenneth Mackenzie, and four children were born to their union: sons Murdoch and Alexander and daughters Sybilla and Margaret. The elder son, destined not to follow his father's footsteps as either a fighting man or farm manager, took up the medical arts and sailed as ship's surgeon on a merchant ship soon lost at sea. Of the two daughters we know that Sybilla married a Glasgow merchant and Margaret a captain in the British navy. Sadly, we know little of their mother, except that she is generally believed to have died before 1774, the year Alexander and some of his kin prepared to sail for New York to join Kenneth's brother John Mackenzie and Isabella's brother John Maciver, the successful cash-paying "Ready Money John," who had gone out to America already and proved the wisdom of such an emigration.

Stornoway had seen many a ship destined for America

with a human cargo. On 14 November 1774 a pair of emigrant ships, used to sailing in company on such a mission
as this, dropped anchor in Stornoway Bay. They arrived to
take on emigrants for America, from the small sandy beach
where the would-be travelers clustered in the hundreds. The
ships bore propitious names: the *Peace & Plenty* and the
Friendship. The former was bound for New York, the latter
for Philadelphia. Alexander was listed as age twelve and,
singularly, as a schoolboy (and not as a servant, like all others
of his age). Some historians have stated that his sisters missed
the boat, being preoccupied with other matters ashore when
the captain made sail. His father is not listed in the emigration papers, but two aunts sailed with him. Alexander Mackenzie was destined for America.

What did Alexander Mackenzie and the other emigrants
carry to America in their characters and education? And
what sort of a life had young Alexander experienced before
he boarded that emigrant ship? We are able to reconstruct
a good deal of what Stornoway was like. "Stornoway and
its people," remarked biographer Roy Daniells with broad
sympathy,

> have for centuries exhibited a mingling of Scottish and English
> traditions and attitudes. Mackenzie's mixed inheritance does
> not fail to embrace Celtic pride, a Highlander's loyalties, the
> self-reliance of the Lewismen. Nor is this found incompatible
> with an equally traditional Scottish caution and foresight. It
> was Mackenzie's good luck that these capacities, combined
> with the Stornowegian instinct for trade, should find a wide
> scope for action in the context of English overseas enterprise,
> which Scots, after the Act of Union, entered into with such
> vigour.

The Isle of Lewis was celebrated for its crofters and fish-
ermen, its spinners and weavers. But in Alexander and his

kin yet another strand was represented, for the Mackenzies were a military family connected to the ancient chief of the Mackenzie clan. If they were to leave their native land, it would be but for awhile, and if forever, then the memory of the home place would be kept alive. As to their education, we can be assured that it was of the highest level that declining circumstances would allow. The earl of Seaforth in earlier days had established a learning institute for children, both boys and girls, where they were taught English, French, and the classics. Alexander Mackenzie, as we have noted, was listed in his emigrant record as a schoolboy, and from this we may conclude that he attended this school. If he did not, his parents would still have given him the best education possible, as they did for his older brother, destined for a career in medicine.

As an adult, Alexander Mackenzie was astute and intelligent, and he showed himself to be widely read and well educated. Like his kin he was a member of the Church of Scotland, which taught hard discipline and independent thinking. Intelligent practicality runs through his writing, as well as a ready understanding of business problems. Stornoway seems to have produced individuals of independent mind and action, self-directed and motivated. Dr. Johnson maintained with wry wit that much might be made of a young Scot, if he were caught young. Such an observation may seem thoughtless, even unkind, but we see its relevance in Alexander's case: he found himself in circumstances largely beyond his own control, and he was soon thrown new challenges that many an older person would not have faced with such adaptable determination.

Mackenzie himself wrote nothing of his early life. In the preface to his *Voyages from Montreal,* however, he wrote poignantly concerning his capabilities for undertaking the arduous demands of northern travel and trade.

I was led, at an early period of life, by commercial views, to the country North-West of Lake Superior, in North America, and being endowed by Nature with an inquisitive mind and enterprising spirit; possessing also a constitution and frame of body equal to the most arduous undertakings, and being familiar with toilsome exertions in the prosecution of mercantile pursuits, I not only contemplated the practicability of penetrating across the continent of America, but was confident in the qualifications, as I was animated by the desire, to undertake the perilous enterprize.

Mackenzie never doubted his own abilities, and seldom, except in the depths of wilderness dejection, did he pause to ponder his problems. Self-pity remained unknown to him, though depression could overcome him. J. B. Tyrrell, himself a celebrated northern Canadian traveler, concluded that Mackenzie was a man of masterful temperament. W. Kaye Lamb, in studying the scholarly literature on Mackenzie, thought otherwise and stated that many indications existed that the explorer was intense and highly strung. Mackenzie was above all resilient. Daily, as we will see, he drove his men forward. He cheered and goaded them. When travel was difficult or Indians threatening, Mackenzie met the dangers with restraint and courage. We can imagine him to have been tough and wiry; in appearance he was blond, strong, and well built.

The portrait of Mackenzie by the king's painter-in-ordinary, Sir Thomas Lawrence, reveals a startling personality. There is in Mackenzie's noble countenance, as captured by the court painter, the burning glow or appearance of *knowing*. Windburned cheeks hint at years of frontier toil. A dimple in the chin gives a youthful impression. Reddish blond hair, unruly and shaggy, frames a broad forehead, immense eyebrows, and remarkably dancing eyes—eyes that show at once intelligence and a look of undoubted success.

This is a face of *surprise,* and of *achievement.* When Macken-zie sat for this portrait and paid Lawrence the going rate of sixty guineas, he was aware that his labors had been crowned with success. He alone, a Hebridean exile, had achieved his goal—to unravel the mystery of the northwest passage—and in doing so had amassed a fortune. He had, indeed, surprised himself. And in coming home to London and Scotland in his latter years, feted and celebrated, he had completed what few Scots were able to do: achieve success at home as well as abroad.

What had the boyhood of this fur trade king been like? Stornoway's past was that of hardship leavened by learning. Games and pastimes are a noted feature of Stornoway children's history. Purpose was not divorced from pleasure with young Alexander. The hard grinding parsimony of Presbyterianism did not consume him. He was as fun-loving and as frolicsome as any of his fellows. Because his mother died while he was still quite young, he would have grown up in close company with his sisters and his aunts. His father and aunts used every means to look after the teenage Alexander. In Canada, too, a lad would be thrust to manhood quickly. Susanna Moodie, noted observer of life in the early colony, commented that there a boy really was a "miniature man—knowing, keen, and wide awake, as able to drive a bargain and take advantage of his juvenile companion as the grown-up, world-hardened man."

In sailing for America, Alexander Mackenzie faced un-imagined difficulties. A land of advertised promise opened to him, as it did to others, and fortunately certain innate abilities, as he himself admitted later, allowed him to pursue a path of success there. At the time, his future lay very much at the whim of colonial politics, brewing revolution, frontier warfare, and imperial will. In sailing from one storm in the Hebrides he was bound for another in North America. What destruction would be left by this storm was not known. Mackenzie and his family, like many others who had fought for king and country, would be placed in another situation requiring the taking up of arms.

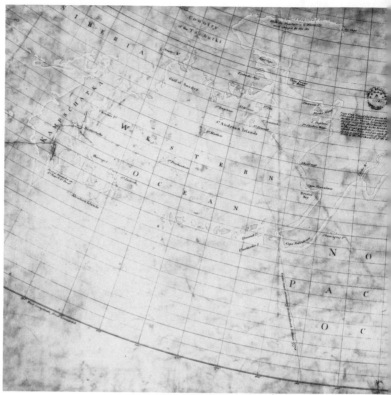

Peter Pond's map showing northern Canada from Hudson Bay to Kamchatka. This copy, dated Athabasca July 1787, is the version he prepared for presentation to the empress of Russia in St. Petersburg. It was never delivered by Pond or his courier Mackenzie. (National Archives of Canada NMC 1161

Aaron Arrowsmith's 1795 map showing new discoveries in northwestern America, including Mackenzie's explorations to the Arctic and Pacific. This copy shows additions to 1814. (National Archives of Canada NMC48909)

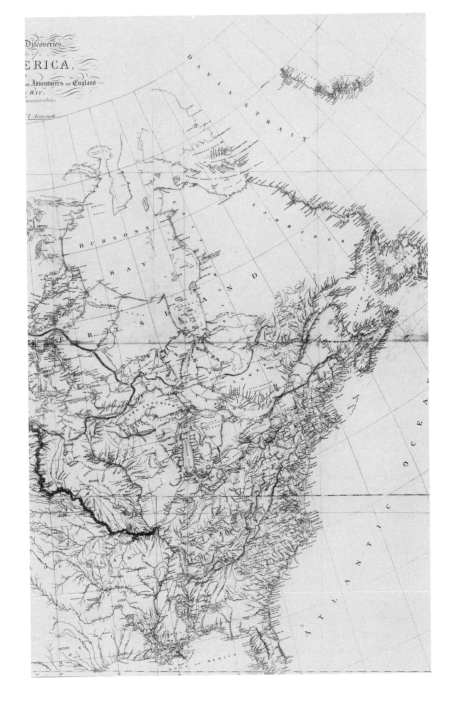

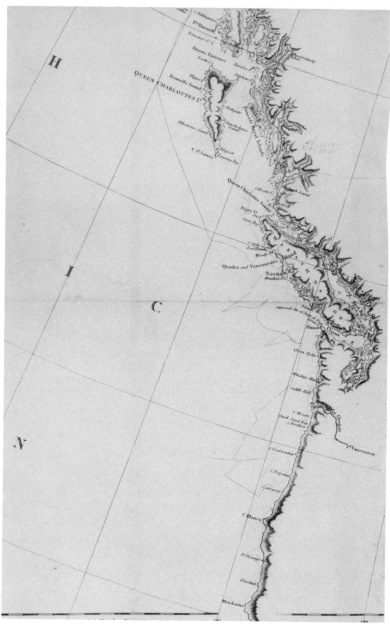

Two portrayals of Mackenzie's far western discoveries as recorded on Arrowsmith's map of North America, 1795 (new edition, 1796). The left panel shows handwritten additions of the location (52°22'N, 129°15'W) where Mackenzie took astronomical observations at the Pacific. Note also Mackenzie's more westerly location of the "Stoney Mountains." The right

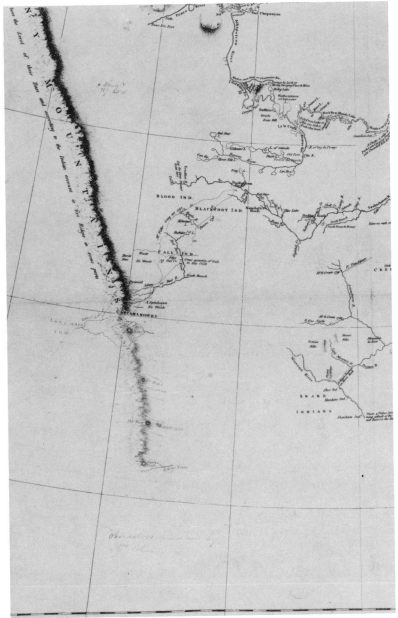

panel shows Mackenzie's 1792–93 winter haven Fort Fork in 56°9'N, 117°45'W. The exploring expedition's track is also marked. Additional discoveries of Rocky Mountains, rivers, and possible passes as far south as 46°30'N are indicated, from information supplied Arrowsmith by Mackenzie through his friend Joseph Colen. (British Library 69917(70))

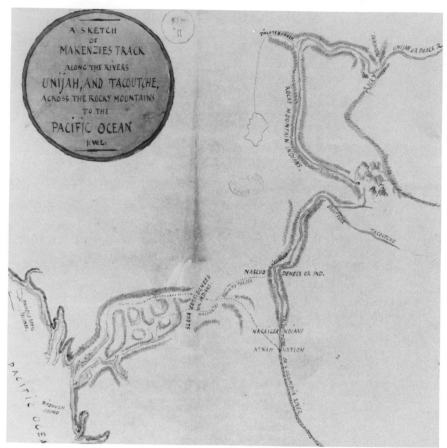

Sketch by Sir James Winter Lake of the Hudson's Bay Company, 1805, showing
Mackenzie's route along the Uninjah (Peace) and Tacoutche (Fraser) Rivers and
then across the Rocky Mountains to the Pacific. Mackenzie mistook the Tacoutche
for the Columbia River. Mackenzie's discoveries worried his rivals in the Hudson's
Bay Company, and this map, adapted from Mackenzie's own map of 1801, was
used by Lake to represent Mackenzie's avenue to the Pacific. (Provincial Archives
of Manitoba HBCA A1/220 fol. 1d N9103)

Sir Alexander Mackenzie in frock coat and lace, pictured here west of the Pacific shores of North America, as shown on the globe. In his right hand are dividers, symbolically representing measurements east and west, north and south. From an undated print by Dye. (British Columbia Archives and Records Service PDP2244)

The Right Honorable.

Henry Addington

Chancellor of the Exchequer &c &c &c &c &c

V O Y A G E S

FROM

from the Author

MONTREAL

THROUGH THE

Continent of North America, &c. &c.

Above, page of presentation copy of Mackenzie's *Voyages from Montreal,* presented by Mackenzie to Henry Addington, chancellor of the Exchequer.

Right, coat of arms of the North West Company, in which Mackenzie rose to prominence. Watercolor by an unknown artist. (National Archives of Canada C8711)

PERSEVERANCE

Joseph Frobisher (1740–1810), a Yorkshireman who was the first European to trade on the Saskatchewan River. He was a great entrepreneur and an original shareholder of the North West Company. Frobisher was in the Canadian West before Alexander Mackenzie's birth. He formed a partnership with Simon McTavish and was thus a rival of Mackenzie throughout the formative years of the North West Company. Like Mackenzie he was, for a time, a politician in the province of Lower Canada. Artist and date unknown. (Metropolitan Toronto Reference Library, J. Ross Robertson Collection T16104)

Alexander Henry the Elder (1739–1824) as portrayed by an unknown artist. Uncle of the noted diarist and trader, and likewise a partner in the North West Company, he was born in New Brunswick, New Jersey, to a merchant family with trading interests in Albany, Detroit, and Montreal. Author of *Travels and Adventures in Canada and the Indian Territories 1760–1776*, he is the unsung hero of a project to search for a northwest passage overland. Although he never made such an expedition, he influenced greatly the actions of others, including his contemporary Peter Pond and, after him, Alexander Mackenzie. (National Archives of Canada C103612)

Simon McTavish (1750–1804), known as "the Marquis" or "the Premier," who dominated the affairs of the North West Company, causing Mackenzie much consternation. A haughty Highlander, McTavish immigrated to America just before Mackenzie and became an original shareholder of the North West Company. Like Mackenzie, McTavish purchased an estate in Scotland, but unlike Mackenzie, he never lived to enjoy the benefits of returning to his native Scotland. After his death Mackenzie took a leading role in the company's affairs. Artist and date unknown. (McCord Museum of Canadian History M1587)

William McGillivray (1764?–1825) as portrayed by an unknown artist. McGillivray became chief director of the North West Company on the death of his uncle Simon McTavish in 1804. He was a contemporary and boon companion of Mackenzie; the two men shared rooms in Montreal and were active members of the Beaver Club. McGillivray and Mackenzie's cousin Roderick helped bring their firm Gregory, McLeod and Company into the North West Company in 1787. McGillivray vigorously opposed Selkirk's buying up of Hudson's Bay Company stock. Mackenzie, however, thought McGillivray failed to take seriously Selkirk's challenge. McGillivray opposed Selkirk's settlement and was arrested by Selkirk at Fort William, Lake Superior. (McCord Museum of Canadian History M18682)

Thomas Douglas (1771–1820), fifth earl of Selkirk, philanthropist and colonial developer, in a portrait attributed to Henry Raeburn. Although younger than Mackenzie, he died in the same year, having engaged in a desperate, crippling struggle with Mackenzie and the Nor'Westers for control of the Hudson's Bay Company and Red River. In 1811, having won majority shareholder status, he sent Miles Macdonell to Red River with Scottish settlers via Hudson Bay. An altruist, he quarreled with Mackenzie about ways and means of empire; settlement ran counter to the interests of the fur trade. (National Archives of Canada C1346)

Edward "Bear" Ellice (1783–1863) as portrayed by Sir William Ross. A London-born merchant banker, fur baron, landholder, and politician, this "fixer" worked the back rooms of corporate London and Montreal. Manipulator of Mackenzie's fortunes in the renegade XY Company, he guided Mackenzie's corporate dealings in "the empire of the beaver," including the reunion with the North West Company in 1804. Intimately connected with the financial and political elite of the British Empire, Ellice eased the merger of the North West Company and Hudson's Bay Company the year after Mackenzie's and Selkirk's deaths. Mackenzie's success owed much to Ellice and vice versa. (National Archives of Canada C2835)

Prince Edward, Duke of Kent (1767–1820), fourth son of George III and Queen Charlotte, in an engraving after a portrait by Sir William Beechey. Prince Edward was a close friend and traveling companion of Mackenzie. For a time commander-in-chief of forces in British North America, he was a well-known figure in Niagara, Montreal, Quebec, and Halifax. Probably on his recommendation, and not on that of Sir Joseph Banks, Mackenzie was knighted. (National Archives of Canada C004297)

Running a rapid on the Mattawa River, c. 1873, in an engraving after a work by Frances Anne Hopkins. All the main explorers of Canada, including Champlain, traveled this river. Mackenzie considered the Mattawa, though short, to be full of rapids and cataracts throughout its length and thus one of the most dangerous of Canadian rivers. This gem of history is today a northern canoeist's delight. (National Archives of Canada C13585)

Canadian voyageurs, the brawn of the northern fur trade, in an engraving after a work by Basil Hall. Superb canoeists, the voyageurs were tough, resilient, hard-drinking men and great lovers of song. These three were attached to Franklin's second expedition and are typical of those whom Mackenzie knew and respected. (National Archives of Canada C9461)

Exploring canoes under sail on Canadian waters, watercolor by George Back, 1821. Mackenzie and his men faced similar perils when crossing Athabasca and Great Slave Lakes. (National Archives of Canada C141501)

Fort Chipewyan on Athabasca Lake, base of Mackenzie's trade and travels, in a watercolor by George Back. Known as the Athens of the North, it boasted a library started by Mackenzie's cousin Roderick Mackenzie. (National Archives of Canada C15251)

Family of Cree hunters at York Fort, similar to many natives of Mackenzie's era, in a watercolor by Peter Rindisbacker, 1821. (National Archives of Canada C1917)

Slave Indians at Fort Providence performing the feather dance, in a watercolor by George Back. Mackenzie witnessed such an event. (National Archives of Canada C141453)

Babtiste E-cho-chi-chu-tho, believed to be a Chipewyan or Métis child, in a lovely portrait by George Back, 1820. Note the snowshoe sketched at the top. (National Archives of Canada C141398)

Buffalo hunt, lithograph by George Catlin, 1844. Natives and Métis provided meat and processed it into pemmican, staple of the fur traders. (National Archives of Canada C100018)

Buffalo meat drying at White Horse Plains, Red River, Manitoba, in 1899, in a watercolor by William Armstrong. (National Archives of Canada C10502)

Place d'Armes, Montreal, 1804, in a watercolor by John Nixon. A familiar location to Mackenzie, Montreal was the commercial and shipping hub of the Canadian fur trade. (McCord Museum of Canadian History, Montreal, M994.89.1)

Mackenzie Rock, British Columbia, two hundred years after Mackenzie's arrival, showing the explorer's message chiseled into the rock at this landmark heritage site. (Photograph by A. M. Robinson)

CHAPTER 2

A Career in the Wilderness

ALEXANDER Mackenzie arrived in New York in early 1775, the same year that the British government was carrying into effect its infamous Quebec Act. That measure aimed to make the province of Quebec into a stronger jurisdiction in the British Empire, complete with an immense interior territory that resembled in its frontier borders New France's vast and ancient hinterland. The Quebec Act, according to its architect, Sir Guy Carleton (later Lord Dorchester, who became one of Mackenzie's strongest supporters), was intended to win the loyalty of the French-speaking, Roman Catholic Canadians, and to make them among the most useful people in advancing the causes of the British Empire. In the Thirteen Colonies widespread complaint arose against this measure, principally on the grounds that Quebec's enlarged western margins, extending the boundaries of the province of Quebec to include the Indian Territory south of the Great Lakes between the Mississippi and Ohio Rivers, stood across the imagined western destinies of Virginia and the Carolinas. In Boston and New York complaints arose that popery had been enshrined on the banks of the St. Lawrence. At the time of Mackenzie's arrival in North America, the continent was on the eve of turmoil, and a year later, in 1776, the Declaration of Independence of the Thirteen Colonies formalized the rising discontent.

In the province of New York in the spring of 1775, with war clouds gathering, Alexander's father Kenneth and his uncle, John Mackenzie, resumed the military careers they had commenced in Stornoway. We do not know when Kenneth Mackenzie arrived in America, but he may have done so in advance of Alexander. Kenneth and John Mackenzie had always fought for the Crown; accordingly, they entered as lieutenants in the King's Royal Regiment of New York, generally known as the Royal Yorks or the Royal Greens. That regiment was raised and commanded by the illustrious Sir John Johnson, himself the son of Sir William Johnson, the sagacious British Indian superintendent whose frontier diplomacy had proved so effective in getting Indians to fight for the Crown against the French. The Johnsons, a sort of family compact, were Indian traders who flourished in the Mohawk Valley of New York, and there, beside Dutch descendants of another empire and among the various Iroquois nations, they maintained a private seat of power that resembled a buffer state between the Thirteen Colonies and Quebec.

Into this enclave the thirteen-year-old Alexander Mackenzie moved from New York City with his two aunts. For a few years he stayed in the Mohawk Valley, near Johnstown, at a place called Sir John's or Scotch Bush. Probably he was a boy soldier, for in those days every able-bodied lad would have been in the militia. Here he would have had his first taste of fighting and of forest diplomacy and woodlands survival. In those fretful times royalists held what they could. Soon, however, the rebels burned their houses and buildings and held Lady Johnson hostage at Johnson Hall.

Mackenzie did not remain in the Mohawk Valley to fight for the king. In 1778, flames of revolutionary war licking all around them, Mackenzie's aunts made plans to escape. They either went to Montreal with their nephew, or sent him on ahead and then followed him to that well-garrisoned safe haven, where he was to attend school. Meanwhile, his father continued to fight in the campaigns of the Royal Yorks. On

7 May 1780, at Carleton Island, near Kingston, Lake Ontario, where his regiment had been sent to garrison the southern frontier of the St. Lawrence against the rebels, Kenneth Mackenzie died, apparently of scurvy. Alexander's uncle, John Mackenzie, attained the rank of captain, survived the war, and took up land grants in Glengarry and Stormont, eastern Ontario, where descendants survive to this day. Alexander's aunts, likewise Loyalists, fell back upon Canada and in 1789 moved to Cataraqui and later to Glengarry.

Like many another soldiering or fur-trading family of Scottish origin, the Mackenzies took Glengarry as their adopted heartland. History is full of coincidences. To Glengarry at this time moved Miles Macdonell, who like Alexander Mackenzie lived under Johnson's protection in the Mohawk Valley. Macdonell and Mackenzie, contemporaries who would have known each other in northern New York, later in life quarreled about the destiny of another heartland—where the forks of the Red and Assiniboine Rivers join. In later years, incidentally, Alexander Mackenzie owned many lands in Glengarry and became a benefactor of the settlements.

Montreal, at the time Alexander Mackenzie arrived in 1778, was half garrison, half port city. The key to the interior trade of the extensive empire of the grand St. Lawrence River, Montreal was where the great commercial classes of Canada had built up their warehouses, offices, townhouses, and shops. Always a place of intense vitality, Montreal was an old French town that the English and Scots had flooded into after the fall of the place in 1760. The fur trade of Canada offered immense wealth, and the English and French both intended to maximize their gains in this avenue of commerce.

In 1779, the year after coming to Montreal, young Alexander Mackenzie entered the world of commerce, specifically the promising fur trade. Such an occupation consisted in the first instance of hard work in the office. If a young man could prove himself in that line, his office work would lead to considerable wilderness travel. Mackenzie, now seventeen, joined the countinghouse of John Gregory, where he would have been put to work as a clerk, filing papers, copying letters, and learning the accounting practices of the age. How Mackenzie came to team up with Gregory we do not know, but he had chosen well. Gregory, an Englishman, had arrived in Montreal only about six years earlier. There he had formed a partnership with a seasoned winter trader turned merchant by the name of John Finlay, who a decade before had boldly pioneered Montreal trade on the Saskatchewan River. Finlay and Gregory forged a remarkable alliance, joining the world of London and Montreal capital with the domain of Saskatchewan frontier commerce. In 1776 Normand McLeod, a discharged Scots soldier, had established himself at Detroit. Upon Finlay's retirement McLeod renewed and rejuvenated the wilderness wisdom of the partnership. Thus, in 1783 the firm became Gregory, McLeod and Company.

These developments occurred precisely when the Treaty of Paris brought the revolutionary war to an end and divided northern North America between British and U.S. jurisdictions. For years afterward the water boundary along the Great Lakes existed only in the imagination, and Canadian fur traders out of Montreal or American traders out of Albany, New York, engaged in cut-throat commerce, bartering arms and liquor for the treasured beaver pelt and other furs. Already in 1783 rivalry among Montreal firms had brought about a confederation under the heading of the North West Company. But the multiyear agreements that held the company together could not contain flamboyant ambition based upon newly garnered wealth and backed by the desire for independence. Mackenzie was one who always worked the margins of this intended monopoly. In those days at Gregory's countinghouse he learned the financial secrets of the business, heard about the rivals, and mastered the details of accounting and shipping. Thus, when he went into the field he had a firm grasp on the particulars of the Canadian fur economy. Future prosperity depended on gathering new information. Fur traders such as Mackenzie contributed mightily to the exploration of the continent. By dint of experience they gathered wide geographical knowledge, especially of river basins, mountain passes, and native peoples. Moreover, their profits as well as their survival depended on the Indians among whom they traveled and traded. They learned about the land's resources and ways to survive in the wilderness. They built trading posts and established networks of communications. Easy as it would be to dismiss these entrepreneurs as unscientific men, more interested in profit than in knowledge, they led lives of the frontier that required a pragmatic disposition. Fur traders engaged in serious gathering of empirical data. Their lives depended on the ability to reach conclusions on the basis of matter-of-fact testing of geographical theorizing. Throughout America's river valleys and mountain passes, fur traders enlarged the world's knowledge about hitherto inaccessible or little known peoples and places. They saw the West, and in Mackenzie's case also the North, as important peripheries of business relationships tied to the banking and warehousing interests of Montreal or New York and to the auction marts and sales rooms of London, Leipzig, Moscow, and Canton. What did they think about "the North" or "the West," a question that now engages students of frontier history? Their opinion of such distant regions was conditioned by the health of their account books, credit arrangements, and future prospects in a cutthroat business.

By the late eighteenth century the fur trade based in Montreal had been in existence for two centuries or more.

Canada was then a country of the canoe. A throughway for birch-bark canoes led inland via rivers and lakes of labyrinthine complexity. Where whitewater advertised disaster for those foolish enough to try to shoot the rapids, back-breaking portages had to be undertaken to circumvent the obstacle. Samuel de Champlain, who laid foundations for New France, had described a watercourse linking the Ottawa and French Rivers westward to Georgian Bay on Lake Huron. Later the French had mastered the trade of the Great Lakes watershed. By 1738 the Canadian-born Pierre de La Vérendrye, employing the Lake of the Woods access, had arrived at the site of present-day Winnipeg and constructed the first fur post on the prairie. Many traders followed him, and after the British conquest of Quebec the rich northern hinterland fell to British control under relentless pressure from the "peddlers from Quebec."

For two decades after the conquest of Quebec, remnants of the ancient French system of fur trade regulation still survived. A variety of regulations, established and enforced by royal authority through the government of New France, devolved to the British province of Quebec. All traders had to possess licenses, furnished by Crown agents, and no person could go northwestward of Detroit without such license, which granted exclusive trade of districts under grants of military commanders. Eventually, individual traders outdistanced the political-military regime anchored at such posts as Detroit, Michilimackinac, and Grand Portage. In the interior, or *le pays d'en haut,* the royal warrant exercised by the British sought to catch up with the aspirations and energies of the successors of the *coureurs de bois.* In this pursuit for the maintenance of law, justice, and authority, they were not always successful.

No matter whether this northern commerce came under French or British dominance, a sort of strange continuity remained as one empire succeeded another. For this branch

of the fur trade was a uniquely Canadian enterprise: it joined
European capital, shipping, and markets with Canadian trading abilities and native hunting and transporting capabilities.
Based in Montreal, then the upper limit of ship navigation
on the St. Lawrence, traders paddled upriver the instant ice
broke up on northern watercourses. They aimed to get as
far inland as possible, into hitherto unexploited fur areas.
In the early years of this trade, seasonal thrusts into the
wilderness were possible. But the fur-bearing wealth of the
forest invariably attracted more and more Canadians, and by
the early eighteenth century new western bases of operation
were required. These were established first at Detroit and
Michilimackinac, and then, by Mackenzie's time, at Grand
Portage at the rocky western rim of Lake Superior.

Grand Portage ranked as the Chicago or Winnipeg of its
day, a transshipping point between East and West. It lay at
the limit of Canadian authority, on the fragile western margins of Quebec's law and order. The commandant, Captain
D. Brehm, reported to the governor of Quebec, Frederick
Haldimand, in 1778 that Grand Portage was a profitable
center for the province of Quebec, because annual proceeds
there were 40,000 pounds sterling and the place employed
500 persons. Every summer at Grand Portage occurred a
rendezvous of about a month's duration. "For the refreshing
and comforting those who are employed in the more distant
voyages," Captain Brehm observed, "the Traders from
hence have built tolerable Houses; and in order to cover
them from any insult from the numerous savage Tribes who
resort there during that time, have made Stockades around
them." A jetty stood below the stockade for receiving goods
brought in from the wider world in schooners and large
Montreal canoes measuring twice the length of the interior
canoes. Warehouses lay at hand for the receiving and storing
of ingoing and outgoing freight.

Grand Portage brought the wintering partners, hardened

by frontier toil, into conjunction with the Montreal partners, seasoned by metropolitan business dealings. The northmen met Montrealers in a spirit of conviviality that can only be imagined, and the *coureurs de bois* were "regaled with bread, pork, butter, liquor, and tobacco." The interior traders derisively dubbed their eastern associates "pork-eaters" because of the fine fare they enjoyed. At these gatherings friendships were renewed, schemes launched, deals made. Here, too, careers were advanced, furloughs arranged, engagements terminated. Talk and gossip flowed fully and eagerly. Besides viewing the marketplace for the sale of furs and the traplines for their production, traders were bound to keep one eye firmly fixed on the state of countinghouses in Montreal and London and the other warily focused on the prospects of the next season's trade. Beyond these concerns lay the external chaotic environment of international affairs, for war with France and the United States could hinder North Atlantic communications and, as it sometimes did, bring ruin to the concern.

Grand Portage served also as a key administrative center for nascent Canadian law in the wilderness. Given its remote location, the place hardly could be said to have any law or justice. In the colonial capital at Quebec, Governor Haldimand worried about how law and order might be better secured in Indian territories. He had trusty information supplied by Captain Brehm acknowledging that among the various interests in the trade, "there must infallibly be some jarring & disputes." The traders ought to be instructed to keep to their own engagements, suggested Brehm, so that disputes between concerns would not arise and violence spread to the interior. The indiscriminate giving of gifts to the Indians ought to end, Brehm advised, and the natives should be warned against interfering with traders. In addition, reports of various councils conducted with the Indians should be transmitted annually to the governor. At this time, routine yearly tours to Michilimackinac of a small military detachment, consisting of an officer and a handful of soldiers, demonstrated the government's resolve to keep peace among the traders and with the Indians.

By 1803 a modicum of law and authority would be established for the Indian or Northwest Territory that lay westward of the new province of Upper Canada, created in 1791 as a Loyalist preserve. In the 1780s, however, arson, murder, and other forms of violence continued intermittently in the interior. The rule of law remained very much that of the wild frontier, with traders contesting among themselves for primacy in the fur business and, in the process, behaving without restraint with regard to the natives.

The talk at Grand Portage may have been about law and order, business and profit. Not far distant, however, lay a different world, where survival was the chief issue. It was known as the North West, that is, the area northwest of Lake Superior. At Grand Portage a back-breaking nine-mile crossing to a navigable river, the Pigeon, brought eastern trading goods and supplies onto the interior water highway, and there the canoes started out along tortuous waterways for the western posts: Rainy Lake, Lake of the Woods, the posts of the Saskatchewan, and those of distant Athabasca. Traders faced constant problems of adequate food supplies, and the farther they roamed from Grand Portage the greater the difficulty. As they advanced from the Lower Saskatchewan to English River and the Upper Churchill, so they required more advanced supply bases: at Lower Winnipeg River, where they stored pemmican, a dried buffalo meat flavored with grease and berries, and at Rainy Lake, Isle-à-la-Crosse Lake, and elsewhere. Ice and shortage of food frequently hindered them from entering new fur preserves, such as that beyond Methye Portage leading to the Athabasca area. Traders who lacked sufficient foodstuffs to winter in dark and freezing northern locations faced terrible hardships. The fur trade offered unlimited possibilities for growth. The boreal forest constituted a rich preserve of mammals, and beaver was the prime fur of the trade. But the land was not uninhabited, and the natives made certain demands on the traders who intruded into it. Traders such as Mackenzie and his contemporary Alexander Henry the Elder depended on meeting native demands in order to push their business successfully in the interior country.

Henry, writing of his experiences in 1775, gave a classic view of trading practices with which Mackenzie would have been familiar. At Lake of the Woods the traders obtained a supply of fish from the local natives and received ceremonial gifts, too. "The mode with the Indians," wrote Henry,

is, first to collect all the provisions they can spare, and place them in a heap; after which they send for the trader, and address him in a formal speech. They tell him, that the Indians are happy in seeing him return to their country; that they have been long in expectation of his arrival; that their wives have deprived themselves of their provisions, in order to afford him a supply; that they are in great want, being destitute of every thing, and particularly of ammunition and clothing; and that what they most long for, is a taste of his rum, which they uniformly denominate *milk*. The present, in return, consisted in one keg of gunpowder, of sixty pounds weight; a bag of shot, and another of powder, of eighty pounds each; a few smaller articles, and a keg of rum. The last appeared to be the chief treasure, though on the former depended the greater part of their winter's subsistence.

The trading practice was invariably orderly and conducted with courtesy and decorum. Doing such business was hard work, for traders found themselves dealing with tough customers. Traders frequently referred to natives as "beggars," by which they meant not that they were necessarily destitute, but that they were capable of making extensive claims against the traders for goods and credit. The whole native village was engaged in trading with the outsiders. Few traders assumed an indifferent attitude. Necessity demanded full bartering, agreements openly arrived at. Rum remained the necessary prerequisite to trade arrangements. The natives demanded rum, but the social costs seldom if ever escaped the traders. Henry, in concluding his narrative of trade relations, remarked: "When morning arrived, all the village was inebriated; and the danger of misunderstanding was increased by the facility with which the women abandoned themselves to my Canadians. In consequence, I lost no time in leaving the place."

A trader could move from place to place, but the logistics of the business required fortified bases of supply and storage. Fur posts of the Northwest, palisaded enclaves built since the early settlement of North America, served as interior headquarters for those who wintered in the wilderness. Within the walls stood a main house for the trader, or *bourgeois*, and in addition there were several storehouses and dwellings. Business was conducted with rigid parsimony, and the records of such transactions came under close scrutiny by partners at the annual rendezvous.

Such native women as lived within the fort's walls were carried on the accounts of the firm, as were their children. Close liaisons with traders were the fashion of the country, and until solemnized marriages became the norm in the 1830s, traders such as Mackenzie kept native women as wives. From these unions, which were advantageous to both trade and diplomacy in the Indian territory, issued interracial families. The descendants of these families became a distinct and important people in Canadian history, the Métis. Sad to say, the record is largely silent about Mackenzie's own native family, which we may nonetheless assume was typical of the families established by fur traders. That traders and native women established close relationships is undeniably true. However, traders often fought against the tendency of "going native" altogether. Alexander Mackenzie's cousin Roderick Mackenzie remarked that the traders became so attached to native ways of life "that they lost all relish for their former habits and native homes." He was speaking of the *coureurs de bois,* the boisterous, gaudy and profligate peddlers who, sporting sufficient credit, arms, ammunition, and guns, gladly left the confines of Quebec for the sexual freedoms and hunting adventures of the *pays d'en haut.* Authorities of New France had tried in vain to counter such tendencies. "This indifference about amassing property, and the pleasure of living free from all restraint," remarked Roderick Mackenzie, "soon brought on a licentiousness of manners which could not long escape the vigilant observation of the missionaries, who had much reason to complain of their being a disgrace to the Christian religion; by not only swerving from its duties themselves, but by thus bringing it into disrepute with those of the natives who had become converts to it; and, consequently, obstructing the great object to which those pious men had devoted their lives." As he explained, "they, therefore, exerted their influence to procure the suppression of these people, and accordingly, no one was allowed to go up the country to traffic with the Indians, without a license from the government."

The Canadian trade in British hands during Mackenzie's time inherited the problems that had beset French authorities before 1763. No missionary force sought to restrict the interior traders, who were accordingly given a free hand. In the circumstances, such concepts of European morals as existed depended solely on the dispositions and determinations of individual traders. Many traders, wrote Roderick, "habituated themselves to the savage life, and naturalised themselves to the savage manners, and, by thus becoming dependant, as it were, on the natives, they acquired their contempt rather than their veneration." Around the 1780s smallpox reached the interior and did its lethal work, reducing all native peoples in numbers and in trading capabilities. Such was the frontier world that Alexander Mackenzie entered. "In the counting house of Mr. Gregory," Mackenzie recollected of these early years of his life, "I had been five years; and at this period [1784] had left him, with a small adventure of goods, with which he had entrusted me, to seek my fortune in Detroit." This riverside city then boomed with commerce, for it was at once, as its French founder Cadillac had realized, the avenue overland to the Mississippi watershed and the access point to Lake Huron and Michilimackinac. Detroit was a place of promise, an English enclave of shipping and mercantile activity. Here the Nor'Westers constructed their upper Great Lakes sloops and schooners, and in the King's Yard the Royal Navy built vessels to show the flag and collect revenue. Here fortunes could be readily made and new careers advanced. A profitable future might have come to young Alexander at Detroit, but a still larger world beckoned.

Mackenzie's prospects now opened up. Exceedingly good fortune befell the young trader at this time, for while he was away in Detroit, Montreal-based Gregory took matters into his own hands as to the young man's future. "He, without any solicitation on my part," recounted Mackenzie, "had procured an insertion in the agreement, that I should be admitted a partner in this business." There was only one condition to be observed by the young clerk: He had to agree to proceed into the Indian country in the following spring, of 1785. Gregory sent his partner Normand McLeod to Detroit to make the proposition.

Not much persuasion was required, for Mackenzie readily assented. He packed his trunks at Detroit and went immediately to Grand Portage to join his associates. Mackenzie had intended fixing upon Detroit to amass his wealth; he was one of many Loyalists who went there at the close of the American revolutionary war. However, the *pays d'en haut* offered richer rewards. He now sported the rank of partner, or *bourgeois,* a Montrealer about to become a frontier trader.

Mackenzie entered a Northwest in which aboriginal peoples had built up pre-European networks from the Canadian shield to Huronia. North America indeed was criss-crossed with native exchange and barter networks, which stretched from the Mississippi to the Arctic and from the Atlantic to the Pacific. Explorer-traders like Mackenzie could only marvel at the extent of these networks and try to tie into them or modify them to their own benefit. Geographical knowledge was key to any advantageous access to the resources of the interior, and that prized knowledge was held by the natives. Mackenzie comprehended this fully. The night before he began his canoe voyage to the Pacific, he scratched in his notes, "Without Indians, I have very little hopes of succeeding."

At Grand Portage those partners that had assembled in 1785 had agreed that John Ross should advance to distant Athabasca, that Mackenzie should proceed to the Churchill River, or English River as it was dubbed, and that Peter Pangman should be stationed at Fort des Prairies for the Saskatchewan district. Alexander's industrious and dedicated cousin Roderick was present at that rendezvous. Roderick's correspondence and career are so significant to our understanding of Alexander's life that more than a word should be said of him here.

Roderick Mackenzie, or Rory as Alexander sometimes referred to him, arrived in Canada in September 1784. First cousin of Alexander Mackenzie, he was about the same age.

Carrying letters of introduction, he too found himself in the healthy, expanding firm of Gregory, McLeod and Company, and thus destined for a career in the interior. Roderick could write well, and the "General History of the Fur Trade" that accompanies Alexander Mackenzie's *Voyages from Montreal* is attributed to him. A keen collector of books and manuscripts, Roderick also made a significant contribution to Canadian letters.

In 1785 Roderick Mackenzie took the then customary passage to the interior by embarking at Sainte Anne, west of Montreal Island, in a brigade headed by a seasoned trader named La Londe. Along the way the canoe flotilla was augmented with John Gregory, Duncan Pollock, James Finlay, Jr., Peter Pangman, James Finlay, Sr., and, west of Michilimackinac, Alexander Mackenzie. Together these men formed one of the dynamic clusters that constituted the North West Company. Alexander and Roderick Mackenzie thus came into the interior trade in the same season, and took leave from Grand Portage for their respective assignments. They kept up a close association, and their correspondence is vital in allowing us to track Alexander's progress.

From Grand Portage in 1785 Alexander Mackenzie went into the southern margins of the Canadian shield. Coursing along its river routes, he reached the Isle-à-la-Crosse area of northwestern Saskatchewan. There he was just over two hundred miles short, as the crow flies, of his future base of operations, Fort Chipewyan. For the present he attended to prosaic duties: keeping accounts, dispatching traders on circuit expeditions to neighboring natives, supervising employees, and, not least, pondering his future enterprises in trade and discovery. He probably took a native wife at this time. Young daughters of chiefs in this country were virtually thrust upon traders, and the linguistic abilities and trading connections of these women marked them out as extremely valuable companions. In 1804 the Fort Chipewyan journal recorded the death of The Catt, Sir Alexander Mackenzie's wife. The Catt must have formed a liaison with Mackenzie sometime around 1785. Perhaps they met at Isle-à-la-Crosse or on the shores of Lake Athabasca. In 1785 Mackenzie held charge of English River. The Indians called that waterway Missinipi, "great river," and Mackenzie shows it on his map by its native name. Canadian fur traders generally gave this waterway the name Churchill River, after the Hudson's Bay Company fort at its mouth. Cree and Chipewyan from present-day northern Saskatchewan and Alberta carried furs down to the Bay traders at Prince of Wales's Fort, or Churchill Fort, on Hudson Bay, established in 1719. Fifteen years before Mackenzie took control at English River, his precursor Joseph Frobisher had intercepted these natives at a place called Frog Portage. He had persuaded them not to go to Churchill Fort, but instead to trade on the spot. Nor'Westers, and their rivals, adopted as policy the cutting off of native trade to the Bay, and Mackenzie adhered to this practice, basing himself at Ile-à-la-Crosse on English River.

Other Nor'Westers traded in and near Mackenzie. But the goings and comings of fellow "peddlers" who went farther north and farther west with the annual hunt for new sources of furs and for new native partners greatly influenced his commercial perspectives at this time. From the headwaters of the Churchill, Peter Pond crossed into the Mackenzie River drainage system in 1778 and opened the pathway to commercial empire that Mackenzie later fully exploited. For the present, however, his time was spent intercepting furs destined for the Bay and building subposts to outflank the works of the great northern rivals.

During his time at Isle-à-la-Crosse and the English River, Mackenzie came to know the English Chief. This native was so named, like the English River, for being leader of those Chipewyan who trekked overland with their furs to the English at Churchill Fort. Post traders there always anxiously awaited the English Chief's appearance, since it promised a bountiful harvest of prime furs. In April 1786, for instance, his arrival with forty men was the largest event of the trade that spring.

Mackenzie called him the English Chief, or Nestabeck. Philip Turnor called him Mis-ta-poose, probably a Cree name. Throughout the fur traders' records Nestabeck makes his appearance, like a firefly making passage through the darkness of history. We find references to him in David Thompson's notes. Surveyor Peter Fidler also met Nestabeck and termed him in 1791 "the Great Chipewyan Chief" Aw-gee-nah. Other traders, James McKenzie among them, speak of successors to the English Chief, who had risen to great prominence. The English Chief dressed richly, in a red greatcoat, short breeches, and common stockings, a style that other Indian leaders aspired to. One such leader was named Marlin, of whom it was said that "he would not be a petty chief, he aspired to be raised from nothing to the highest pitch of Glory which a Mongtagner [native trader] could possibly be raised to."

Had the English Chief written memoirs, what a fascinating tale he could have told of the passages of Europeans throughout the Canadian Arctic and sub-Arctic. The English Chief knew all the northwestern explorers: the English sailor turned trader Samuel Hearne, the noble surveyor Philip Turnor, the grizzled veteran trader Peter Pond, the mapmaker David Thompson, and the manager of Hudson's Bay Company operations Sir George Simpson. Nestabeck saw the trade of the Hudson's Bay Company collapse along the lakes and rivers of Saskatchewan. He had accompanied Matonabbee when he guided Hearne from the shores of Hudson Bay to the Coppermine River. When Nestabeck arrived at Athabasca in 1786, a jubilant Pond clothed him in garments befitting his powerful influence.

In 1789 the English Chief would seem the natural native guide and leader to accompany Mackenzie on his thrust toward the Western Sea. But even while Mackenzie was still conducting the prosaic trade at Ile-à-la-Crosse, he was already learning about the native alliances and power relations. Mackenzie did not discover the English Chief; it was the other way round. Together they forged an alliance that brought both of them power and influence. Few combinations of European and native were more powerful than this one, and to the end of his days Mackenzie sang the praises of the English Chief as the one man who knew the most about safe, successful travel in the wilds of northern Canada.

As Mackenzie remarked, he had no hope of succeeding without native guides. The English Chief was one such reliable guide, and Mackenzie must have wished on more than one occasion that he had more such. Native guides were often multilingual and could be superb interpreters. Their geographical knowledge, however, did not always extend beyond their region. Distant knowledge was something of report—that is to say, in need of confirmation by on-the-ground reckoning. Fur traders provided such empirical data and often made them known to a world wider than that of their own immediate commercial concerns.

The local nature of much native geographical knowledge does not detract from its value. What is significant is the use made of such knowledge. Natives knew the land as home—as a place for hunting and fishing, as a sacred place. Europeans like Mackenzie saw rivers and lakes as tributaries of commerce, mountains and terrain as obstacles to be surmounted. At the same time, they valued the land as the source of the desirable furs they wished to obtain from the natives.

CHAPTER 3

The River of the West and the Western Sea

VISIONS of promoting a Canadian "Adventure to China" gathered momentum in the 1760s, shortly after Canada fell under British control by the Peace of Paris (1763). Projections of opening up a great commerce with Asia were still current in Mackenzie's era. As exploration advanced, however, schemes became narrower in scope and more defined in purpose.

In 1768 the governor of Quebec, Sir Guy Carleton (later Lord Dorchester), advised the senior statesman in London in charge of trade policy, Lord Shelburne, that British traders from Montreal should proceed across the continent to the Pacific Coast. There, Carleton reckoned, they would "find out a good port, take its latitude, longitude, and describe it so accurately as to enable our ships from the East Indies to find it out with ease, and then return the year following." Carleton had in mind a government-authorized expedition in which the traders would go up the Western Lakes, as was customary, and then winter in one of their distant posts before setting out again early in the spring for the Pacific Ocean. Here was a concrete proposal, perhaps the first, for trans-Pacific trade based upon the St. Lawrence. Twenty-five years later Mackenzie carried out a similar project, but he did so entirely by his own arrangement.

Similar schemes involving a search for a northwest passage by sea and land, as well as the founding of a base of operations near the mouth of the Strait or Straits of Anian, were then being trumpeted by persons such as Major Robert Rogers, Jonathan Carver, and Alexander Henry the Elder. Rogers sought British government funds for finding his river of the West, the "Oregan," which he claimed flowed from near Mississippi headwaters to the western ocean. Carver, hired by Rogers, journeyed into Minnesota and made a great circuit trip that yielded no favorable result. Still, he held that a British settlement on the northwest coast of North America would encourage trade, discovery, and communication with China and English trading settlements in the East Indies. Carver was something of a visionary, and he had gone so far as to say that there was a river of the West, the River Oregon, that rose "in about the center of this great continent" and flowed into the Pacific Ocean. This insight derived from information gleaned from natives. The river of the West appeared on a French map prepared by the explorer Baron Lahontan in 1709. A *mer de l'Ouest* (western ocean) likewise decorated charts of the continent. These seemingly wild imaginings needed proof, which Alexander Henry intended to provide.

Henry set about to become the true architect and planner of a transcontinental expedition of science and trade that would be the best of its day. Linked as he was to Sir Joseph Banks, the British scientist and "fixer" of exploration, Henry hoped to unlock the secrets of the interior of North America. However, it fell to others to complete the task. While Henry launched a scheme of discovery, pathfinders such as Peter Pond, Alexander Mackenzie, David Thompson, and others less well known pushed back the bounds of empirical knowledge. Such bold, even wild ideas of geography and equally spacious visions of empire and wealth had to be tested—by tedious hours at canoe paddles and by long, back-breaking days on foot. These men did not wait patiently for government authorization and funding; they pressed on independently, actively seeking what armchair geographers and desk-bound strategists mused about in snug surroundings. Mackenzie went into Athabasca hard on the heels of Pond, and his life provides a remarkable counterpoint to the older man's. Pond deserves much more credit than Mackenzie would admit. Pond's life is instructive about the logistical problems the explorers faced and the commercial strategy that Mackenzie exploited and profited by. Born in 1739, son of a Connecticut shoemaker and descendant of an old colonial line of military men, Peter Pond eagerly took up arms for King George III, fighting against French forces at Ticonderoga, Fort Niagara, and Montreal. His military campaigning led Pond to take a favorable view of Canada and its prospects at the Peace of 1763. However, as he wrote in his narrative, in consequence of the conquest of Quebec, there was evidently "no business left for me in Canada." He took up seafaring as a profession but decided to enter the fur trade. Of industrious habits and with a good common education, he was a feisty, roistering, self-directed man who took to trading with the native people as easily as he campaigned in wilderness military forays. Of a violent temper and perhaps morose and quarrelsome disposition, he often picked fights with rivals; twice, or so it is alleged, he committed or plotted murder or manslaughter against other traders. Both times he ran free in a wild world where the writ of the Crown in Canada had only paper authority.

For a short time, family obligations kept Pond relatively close to home. In 1765 he was sufficiently free to begin life as a trader at Detroit, working in conjunction with those based at Albany, an important location for shipments of goods into the interior via the Hudson River and nearby waterways. Running south of the St. Lawrence River system, this conduit of American trade used by the Alexander Henrys (Elder and Younger) and others circumvented some of the obstacles of the northern river route—much as in the mid-nineteenth century the Erie Canal subverted the old St. Lawrence canal system. Fast-growing Detroit became the advance interior headquarters for this trade, while Grand Portage and Michilimackinac on Lake Superior, and Prairie du Chien, where the Wisconsin flows into the Mississippi, provided inland springboards to the Old Northwest. For a decade Pond roamed this vast quarter, bringing bulging cargoes of trade goods to the natives. Increasingly skilled in the subtle ways of dealing with the native peoples, he was on one occasion employed by fellow traders as a diplomat to arrange a peace between the Dakota and Chippewa. He was the first to provide ethnographic descriptions of the Yankton Dakota.

In the 1770s the trade of the Old Northwest remained unappealing to investors, and the commerce at Detroit earned a reputation as dull, bad, or indifferent, for French and Spanish traders from the Mississippi frequently undersold the English. A future of great wealth did not lie here. The upper Mississippi could not contain the redoubtable Pond. Besides which, British traders were now shifting northward into the western limits of the Great Lakes system. Detroit, the western haven for Loyalists during the American War of Independence and the business base of the Old Northwest, had long been a French trading post, but now, in the buoyant era of Pond and Mackenzie, it was a fulcrum of British, Canadian, and American western commerce that reached north and west via waterways to Michilimackinac, Sault Ste. Marie, St. Joseph, and Grand Portage. The region was still an open frontier. Some Spanish traders from Louisiana had plundered and destroyed Michilimackinac in 1781. Twelve years earlier an observer at St. Joseph remarked that "traders from Montreal, traders from the other side of the Mississippi, and the Lord knows from where" roamed at large. Traders representing various interests passed through the area at will.

In 1775 Pond decided to extend his successful trade. His route lay inland of the "lakehead," as it then was, at Grand Portage. Known to the French since the early eighteenth century and thoroughly exploited by them, this base had seen numerous English and Scottish traders from Montreal in the decade or so after the conquest of Canada. Indeed, one observer, shortly before the termination of hostilities, marveled that the fur routes of the Northwest were "as thick as Mosquitos" with English traders. Merchants from Montreal, such as James Finlay in 1767 and Thomas Curry in 1771, were pathfinders on the Saskatchewan River, the great artery of the prairie West. Joseph Frobisher and Alexander Henry the Elder followed. They advanced farther than either of their predecessors, setting up posts among Athabasca Indians, who told them of a Peace River draining from the Rocky Mountains beyond which, at not a great distance, lay a salt lake, the Pacific.

Pond, first among equals, went into the interior in late 1775 accompanied by other Canadians bent on peddling wares in untapped areas. Even this early Pond had acquired a reputation, as Alexander Henry the Elder observed, that had given him some "celebrity" in the Northwest. Pond's aggressive trading practices had earned him a reputation as someone not to be antagonized, as he had a tendency to take the law into his own hands.

Pond wintered at Lake Dauphin, in central Manitoba, where he intercepted Indians bound for the recently erected Hudson's Bay Company post at The Pas, known as Cumberland House. Pond was beating the company at its own game, for it had put up the Pine Island post to cut into the Nor'Westers' lifeline of trade and to attract native trade to its own post. Pond managed to bypass the customary means of stationary trade that the Hudson's Bay Company had brought to the interior, and he was taking the business to new frontiers of influence. The successful early years in this region soon attracted the attention of fellow agents based at Grand Portage. At this time—1778, according to Mackenzie, who had evidence of this directly from Pond—several traders who had goods to spare put them into common stock. The trading interests in this new partnership gave the management of the enterprise to Pond. They instructed him to enter the Churchill River and probe the heart of the Athabasca country, then only known to the "peddlers" by reports that had reached them from natives. This new arrangement constituted the direct forerunner of the North West Company. By the association of capital, the minimizing of competition, the sharing of risk, and the pursuit of a common commercial objective, the traders established a profitable monopoly. Otherwise, endless feuds would have ensued, diminishing profits.

In late 1778 Pond crossed into the Athabasca watershed from the lakes and rivers of the Saskatchewan and Churchill. Perhaps Indians told him the way there, or he may have followed a well-worn native trail. In any event, before winter he came upon a thirteen-mile portage over the height of land between northwestward-flowing and eastward-coursing streams. The scene was majestic beyond imagining; Mackenzie's *Voyages from Montreal* describes it as follows: "Within a mile of the termination of the portage a very steep precipice . . . rises upwards of a thousand feet above the plains beneath it, [and] commands a most extensive, romantic, and ravishing prospect."

Pond's discovery marked the first known crossing of the La Loche or Methye Portage by a trader, and its significance as a new northern gateway was tremendous. From this key to Athabasca country, a new world awaited the fur trader well stocked with trading goods and food supplies. To his delight Pond found Cree and Chipewyan eager to trade. By penetrating into the Athabasca wilderness and opening its trade, Pond and others diverted furs from the untrapped Northwest to Montreal, drawing a ring around their Hudson's Bay Company competitors.

Pond set up his winter post, which Mackenzie called Pond's House, on Elk River, about forty miles south of Athabasca Lake, or Lake of the Hills as it was then called. This establishment, Mackenzie stated, was the only one in this part of the world until 1785. Wintering there in 1778–79, Pond saw, in Mackenzie's words, "a vast concourse" of Cree and Chipewyan tribes bound on their annual excursion to Fort Churchill on Hudson Bay by way of the long and difficult route to saltwater. These tribes were delighted to see Pond, for by trading with him they could avoid a long, troublesome journey. Prepared to accept less than they would have received at Fort Churchill, they happily made their deals on the spot. By this arrangement Pond unlocked the secret of the little known distant trade of the Athabasca and Peace River watersheds. Not least, he had stopped much of the Hudson's Bay Company trade near its source.

The North West traders now reaped rich trading rewards. Like Radisson and Groseilliers north of Lake Superior in the 1650s, who were "Caesars of the wilderness," Pond found no one to challenge his trade. He came heavily laden out of Athabasca that next spring of 1779 and let slip boastfully to a Hudson's Bay Company factor at Cumberland House, William Walker, that he had gone far enough north to trade with Matonabbee and the Northward Indians. Pond hastily returned to Athabasca to bring out a second cache of prime furs and soon, in discussions with others, laid the basis of a grand fur trade strategy of the West.

Others watched Pond's success with envious eyes. The sagacious Alexander Henry the Elder, a peddler from New Jersey who traded from Albany and Montreal through De-

troit, immediately grasped the significance of this. He oppor-
tunistically pressed upon Sir Joseph Banks of the Royal
Society of London an account of the benefits that would
accrue to British science and empire if an exploratory expedition were to be mounted, with Henry in command, to open
a new transcontinental route of commercial importance.
The scheme died away, but was revived in the designs that
Mackenzie later advanced.

If Henry appropriated Pond's findings without acknowledgment, and if Mackenzie likewise failed to give sufficient
credit to the pioneering Pond, we must recognize that specific ownership of ideas and schemes was almost unheard
of in their day. Indeed, the public speculated rather wildly
on possibilities of commercial growth by new schemes. A
cursory reading of pamphlet literature dealing with the aims
of British imperial thinkers of the day with regard to Canadian affairs will reveal the freewheeling approach of the
would-be architects of profit and power. As part of this
trend, the principal men engaged in the Athabasca trade
headed by Pond forged a new partnership in 1783, the North
West Company of Montreal.

At about this time Pond's problems mounted in earnest.
The death of Jean-Étienne Waddens, an affair that Pond
may have been involved in, resembled corporate warfare, a
way to get rid of a well-placed rival. Waddens, "a Swiss
gentleman, of strict probity and known sobriety," as Mackenzie described him, rivaled Pond too closely. "Two men,
of more opposite characters, could not, perhaps, have been
found." Ill-will became the order of the day. Waddens was
shot by Pond or by one of his own clerks. Even as Pond
was eagerly preparing memoranda and maps to buttress his
claims to a new fur empire with limitless possibilities, forces
were acting against him. During his third winter in Athabasca, 1783–84, Pond was able to question natives about
northern waters, especially Great Slave and Great Bear Lakes.

Like Mackenzie he had a larger vision. He learned something of the courses of the Peace and Mackenzie Rivers. In 1785 Pond was among a group of Montreal traders who signed a memorial urging the Governor Haldimand to support a scheme for discovery of these northwestern reaches under Pond's leadership.

The geographical riddle that Pond and his associates sought to solve had been suggested by Captain James Cook of the Royal Navy. In 1784–85 Pond read or learned of narratives of Cook's voyage to the North Pacific, possibly William Ellis's presumably authentic (though unauthorized) preview of Cook's reconnaissance, published in 1782. Cook had named Cook's River (now Cook Inlet near present-day Anchorage, Alaska) as a body of westward-flowing water. Pond speculated, quite incorrectly though understandably, that this was a conduit linking the Pacific with a great lake or river of Athabasca or lands to the north. In one of the rudimentary maps that he prepared for the U.S. Congress, dated 1 March 1785, Pond showed rivers and lakes proceeding westward from the Great Lakes and Hudson Bay to the Rocky Mountains and northward to the Arctic. On a surviving copy of this map, a note states that "from his own discoveries as well as from the reports of Indians [Pond] assures himself of having at least discovered a Passage to the N[ord] O[uest] Sea." But Pond changed various details of his map to suit circumstances, and his preparation of some versions for the government of the United States hardly sat well with Canadians and Britons who feared the sale of official secrets.

Still, the power of Pond's vision was not easily quelled. Governor Henry Hamilton of Canada was anxious to support Pond and to keep him in the imperial network, thus preventing him from aiding the United States or any other country, such as Russia. Hamilton urged the British government to support the Nor'Westers. In due course the British organized such an expedition, as Henry the Elder and Pond had separately proposed, and ordered Captain John Frederick Holland, a surveyor and engineer, to command the exploring expedition. However, this project was canceled in the fall of 1790 when news reached Quebec and Montreal that, almost unannounced, the young and unknown Alexander Mackenzie had explored the Mackenzie River to its mouth and found its course very different from what Pond had proposed.

From that moment, Pond's star faded rapidly and that of Mackenzie glowed ever brighter. Pond departed Athabasca for good in the spring of 1788, leaving the field to Mackenzie. The murder of Waddens and the death of another trader, John Ross, led to Pond's forced retirement. Pond found himself dropped from the North West Company. He redoubled his activities south of the border and toyed for a while with the establishment of rival arrangements. Like other traders, he distrusted inquisitive visitors. When a frontier trader from Montreal called upon Pond in later years, he found him at dinner with companions. A startled Pond jumped to his feet, seized a carving knife, and swore he would stab the first man that touched him. "Oh!" cried the trader, "I do not come to arrest you, but only to have a little fur gossip." "I do not believe you," replied Pond. "The sooner you leave the room the better for you." The visitor took the hint. In his late years Pond waged a war of secrecy against his enemies, real or imagined. He is known to have advised the American boundary commissioners on where the Great Lakes border ought to be in order to benefit American interests. In the end he may have gained retribution against rival traders and British schemers of empire. But he did not fare well financially. Pond died penniless in 1807 in his native Milford, Connecticut.

Unlike Pond, who died in poverty, Alexander Mackenzie grew rich on the profits of Athabasca, with scant thanks to

Pond's preliminary findings. Mackenzie dissociated himself, indeed rapidly distanced himself, from Pond, whose hands were bloodied and whose cartography was flawed. Such a position is understandable, for his own early life had been disrupted by similar discord. But Pond opened what Mackenzie and others called the "new el dorado" of the North West Company. The new fortunes of Mackenzie and the Montrealers revolved around the discoveries of the La Loche Portage and of the Athabasca River and Lake Athabasca—both attributed to Pond. Pond's handling of logistics was exemplary; in particular, his careful use of supplies, including pemmican, and his good organization were keys to success. He set a feverish pace of travel and established an enviable record of voyaging along routes of the continental interior. Pond was the first to outline the general features of the upper Mackenzie River system, and his findings had important consequences for Mackenzie. A ready learner, Mackenzie profited from Pond's pioneering enterprises and geographical suggestions and went on to build a career and reputation on business activities and commercial expansion suggested by Pond. Pond's findings fired the young Scot with the possibilities of discovery in the Mackenzie River watershed and led to Mackenzie's decision to follow the course of the great river to the sea in 1789.

At the time of Pond's greatest notoriety and success in the *pays d'en haut,* Mackenzie was first being noticed by the wider world. A person of scientific inquiry in Montreal, Judge Isaac Ogden, mentioned Mackenzie in a letter to his father, David Ogden, in London on 7 November 1789. Judge Ogden began by telling his father that he had met Pond, "a Gentleman of observation and Science," who, rather than just speculating on the distances between important places, had actually traversed many of the interior territories. Pond's map, which found its way into the prestigious pages of the 1790 *Gentleman's Magazine,* revealed to the wider public

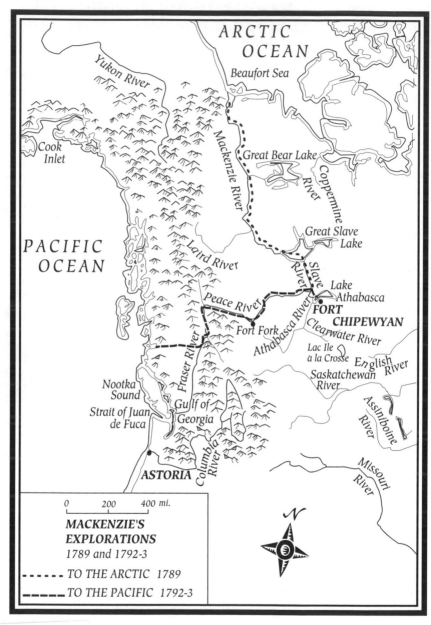

ARCTIC
OCEAN

Beaufort Sea

Yukon River

Cook Inlet

Mackenzie River

Great Bear Lake

Coppermine River

PACIFIC
OCEAN

Great Slave Lake

Laird River

Slave River

Peace River

Lake
Athabasca

**FORT
CHIPEWYAN**

Fort Fork

Athabasca River

Clearwater River

*Lac Ile
à la Crosse*

English River

Saskatchewan River

Fraser River

Assiniboine River

*Nootka
Sound*

*Strait of Juan
de Fuca*

*Gulf of
Georgia*

Columbia River

Missouri River

ASTORIA

0   200   400 mi.

**MACKENZIE'S
EXPLORATIONS**
1789 and 1792-3

• • • • • *TO THE ARCTIC 1789*

——— *TO THE PACIFIC 1792-3*

N

zie's explorations of 1789 and 1792–93.

the trade route from the upper end of Lake Superior to the waters communicating with the northwestern interior. A chain of lakes brought British traders both north of the Mississippi and south of Hudson's Bay Company interests. Ultimately the waters of this northwestern course led to a great lake called Slave Lake, "the last water before you come to the Great Northern Ocean . . . where the water ebbs & flows, of which the Gentleman gave me indubitable proofs." The Montrealer pressed upon the Londoner the importance of the following details: "The Lakes that empty into the Great Slave Lake, at least the largest of them are named the Arabaska [Athabasca] (which has a large River running into Slave Lake of three or four hundred miles at least in length, its course North West). . . . The River that carries all these Waters into the Slave Lake is called Slave River and is very large, it runs North West several hundred miles in Length." Now Judge Ogden warmed to the geographic possibilities of discovery. "From out of the Great Slave Lake runs a very large River, which runs almost South West, and has the largest Falls on it in the known World." This statement was a falsehood, and so was that which followed: "The great chain of Mountains that extend from Mexico along the Western or Pacific Ocean, and the Northern Pacific Ocean, terminates in Lat. 62½ & Longitude 136, so that the Slave River runs to the Westward of them and empties into the Ocean by its course in about Lat. 59." If that had been true, which it was not, a waterway would have led to the Pacific at about the latitude of present-day Anchorage, Alaska, which was then placed on nautical charts under the title "Cook's River." The judge urged his father to look at his maps: "When you have proceeded thus far, & you have looked over your map," he instructed with uncompromising certainty, "you will readily conjecture what River the above Slave Lake River is known by, when it empties into the

Ocean. To save you much Trouble I will tell you it is Cook's River."

Judge Ogden in Montreal had no doubts of the veracity of Peter Pond's arguments, and he was clearly impressed by the details Pond had given him in conversation. For instance, he noted that Cook had found a great deal of driftwood on the northwest coast, that only on the banks of the river that emptied into Slave Lake could wood be found, and that the river in question was the only one leading to the Pacific. Besides, Pond had met two natives who came up that river all the way to Slave Lake. "They brought him in 1787 a Blanket which they received from Vessels which were at the Mouth of the River; they say that the River he was in is large to the place of Discharge and Navigable, so that if we take the Latitude and Longitude of the two Rivers, the Courses, and all the other circumstances into consideration, little doubt remains that they are the same." To the north the traders met "Esquimaux Indians," or Inuit, whom they found as far north as was known. Ogden speculated that if Captain Cook had ventured into these waters from the Pacific in the right season, in the middle of September he might easily have returned to Europe by a passage along the northern coast of America.

Ogden drew several conclusions from Pond's claimed discoveries and prospects, and the most telling for Mackenzie's future scheme ran as follows: "That an easy communication with, and an advantageous commerce may be carried on by Posts established on Lakes Slave, Arabaska, Pelican, &c &c., and to deliver the Fruits of their commerce at the Mouth of Cook's River, to be then carried to China &c., and that as Cook's River and the Lands on Slave Lake, Arabaska &c. are very fine, some advantageous settlements many be made there which may be beneficial to Government." And he noted a further, strategic value: "Perhaps another use might be made in time of War by this Route, which would be to convey Intelligence to the East Indies by that Route."

In these musings Ogden spelled out the hoped-for particulars of the Canadian dream: a navigable northwest passage of commercial, settlement, and military value. He was playing on the grand and venerable theme, promoted in its new form by Peter Pond, to bring British dominion and trade to Pacific shores and China by way of northwestern America. This letter, which closes with an important reference to Alexander Mackenzie, contains the first outside, or nontrading, mention of the future explorer: "Another man [,] by the name of McKenzie[,] was left by Pond at Slave Lake with orders to go down the River, and from thence to Unalaska, and so to Kamchatka, and thence to England through Russia &c. If he meets with no accident you may have him with you [in London] next year."

Judge Ogden's fascinating report from Montreal soon came to the attention of the government, and with it news that Mackenzie might be destined for Russia. David Ogden presented his son's account of Pond's explorations of the interior parts of North America to none other than the Rt. Hon. W. W. Grenville, a senior member of the British cabinet and a strong promoter of trade and empire. Grenville held successively in these years a number of key posts. This statesman and his associates in London were then pondering the possibilities of such a northwest passage, for Captain Cook's northwest coast explorations, though valuable in themselves, had left yawning gaps in the chart of the shoreline. Besides, several private traders, including James Hanna, James Strange, John Meares, and Charles Duncan, were by their commercial pursuits yielding more geographical information of a reliable kind than Cook had reported in his cursory reconnaissance.

Alexander Dalrymple, hydrographer of the East India Company and preeminent in his knowledge of Pacific cartography, pressed upon the government the urgent necessity of a government-sponsored expedition to get to the "backside of America," as the Elizabethans had put it, and learn the truth of these speculations. "The present object of Discovery is *De Foucas's Strait* in 48 ½ N. Lat.," stressed Dalrymple, "and if they can find a convenient harbour on that Coast to winter in, much progress may be made by land during the winter towards effecting a communication; and if they choose they can proceed to the Sandwich Islands & return at the early part of Spring." He urged an exploratory expedition via Hudson Bay in preference to one around Cape Horn. The work of Captain Cook was now being called to account, and Dalrymple put it delicately but forcefully: "The ancient idea of a N.W. Passage was by the Hyperborean Sea on the N. of America, altho' I am very far from meaning any imputation on Capt. Cook's memory or abilities, I cannot admit of a *Pope* in Geography or Navigation."

Dalrymple maintained that a northwest passage existed. He did so on several grounds: linguistic affinities of natives at both east and west extremities of the northern coast of the continent, the absence of timber in high latitudes, and the overlapping evidence of documentary accounts and maps. All these pointed to the existence of a sea route. This famous geographer, who had a friend in George Wegg, governor of the Hudson's Bay Company, dismissed Pond's discoveries as inaccurate and untrustworthy. Dalrymple was accordingly sympathetic to the company's plea that government should provide "two proper persons" to travel inland to "ascertain the shortest communication by the Lakes & Rivers." The Hudson's Bay Company was willing to defray reasonable costs of the undertaking and to provide a sloop for exploratory purposes, should government agree to the scheme. Soon a grand scheme was got up. Plans called for an overland exploratory party to include a surveyor and his assistant, four boatbuilders, eight Canadians, and native canoemen. Detailed instructions were readied for required supplies, scientific instruments, and other necessities needed to discover the area lying between Lake Athabasca and the coastline examined by Cook.

We cannot leave this planning for an exploratory expedition without mentioning Dalrymple's caustic assessment of Pond. Dalrymple remained suspicious of Canadian traders and favored the Hudson's Bay Company (in particular, he noted that the intended discoverers would profit best from information to be obtained by astronomer and surveyor Philip Turnor, who had already set out for Lake Athabasca). He could not control his distrust of Pond, concerning whom he wrote, "Supposing some person of knowledge and veracity to be sent with him it is probable Pond would *hide* that Person as is at present alleged of a person whose merits raised his Jealousy." By this Dalrymple, who was fond of cloaking his own imperial schemes in mystery, meant that Pond would do all in his power to gain preeminence of discovery and the fruits of new geographical frontiers. To this Dalrymple added a decisive closing line that killed Pond's hopes: "It is also to be considered that Pond is a native of the United States, and cannot therefore be deemed to be attached to this Country. He also pretends to the Sovereignty of the Lands adjacent to the Arathapeskow Lake [Great Slave Lake], so that by encouraging him we may be fostering a viper in our bosom."

What led Dalrymple to such an assessment can only be imagined; certainly there was at work a network of backstairs informants determined to cut Pond out of the trade. Pond's violent reputation had preceded him, and neither the North West Company nor the British Empire held any future for him. Peter Pond, who had fought for the king in the Seven Years' War, played a brief, though brilliant, role in the exploration of North America. Pond was a great man in his own right, one who served for a time as the gatekeeper to those remarkable secrets soon opened to the wider world by Mackenzie—secrets that ended the necessity of government sponsorship for an elaborate expedition such as had been got up in council chambers and clubs in London. First north, then west, Mackenzie with a handful of men revealed the principal secrets of the far interior that had mystified so many and had perplexed geopolitical thinkers for three centuries.

While governments in Quebec and London pondered the possibilities of northwestern discovery and mulled over the merits of Pond's inquiries, Mackenzie was already well ahead. In 1787, the year before Pond's precipitate departure, Mackenzie arrived in Athabasca as Pond's successor. He crossed Portage La Loche in late autumn, on 11 October of that year. This was the first of ten portages he was to make over this celebrated division between waters emptying into Hudson Bay and those flowing into the Arctic. During that winter of 1787–88 Pond undoubtedly gave Mackenzie all the necessary information and inspired him with the possibilities of discovery. Mackenzie's journey became the fulfillment of Pond's plans. By January 1788 Mackenzie had become convinced that an expedition would be profitable. To his cousin Roderick he confided, "I already mentioned to you some of my distant intentions. I beg you will not reveal them to any person as it might be prejudicial to me, though I may never have it in my power to put them in execution."

Meanwhile, Mackenzie maligned Pond's scheme. Maliciously he sought to claim it for himself. In a letter written by his superior Patrick Small, dated 24 February 1788, there is mention of "the wild ideas Mr. Pond has of matters, which Mr. Mackenzie told me were incomprehensibly extravagant—He is preparing a fine map to lay before the Empress of Russia."

About this same time Roderick observed that Alexander

"became extremely anxious and uncertain whether he would leave or remain in the country." For reasons that are not given, Alexander Mackenzie decided to remain in Athabasca. Most likely Pond's exit from the interior gave Mackenzie a new opportunity, one he longed for. He hated idleness above all. Before the end of July he was back at Rainy Lake, or Lac la Pluie, where he arranged for the pressing supply requirements of the Athabasca. He insisted that Roderick, still trading at Churchill River, accompany him into far Athabasca. Despite his high regard for his cousin, however, Roderick would not go. Mackenzie, in a quandary, had now no alternative but to show his hand and to reveal his plan. Then it dawned upon Roderick that his cousin was fretting about the problems of exploration. Roderick put it this way in his *Reminiscences:*

> He then informed me, in confidence, that he had determined on undertaking a voyage of discovery the ensuing Spring by the water communications reported to lead from Slave Lake to the Northern Ocean, adding, that if I could not return and take charge of his department in his absence, he must abandon his intentions. Considering his regret at my refusal, and the great importance of the object he had in view, I, without any hesitation, yielded to his wishes, immediately set to work and accompanied him into Athabasca.

Alexander Mackenzie now enjoyed trusty support to manage the affairs of Athabasca in his absence, full authority to complete a rapid reorganization of the posts of the area, and complete freedom to undertake his mission into unknown parts. Free of the pressing executive obligations that had pinned him down for a decade, he was released to pursue the northwest passage.

For the moment, pressing business matters demanded attention. Fort Athabasca, or "Mr. Pond's Old Establishment," remained for a while the base of operations and explorations for the Mackenzie cousins. Alexander's design called for a reordering and expansion of posts. Inexorably, the mechanisms of the fur business drew the traders ever northwestward.

Roderick selected a site for the new depot on Lake Athabasca. He chose a "conspicuous projection," now Old Fort Point, on the southern side of the lake, some eight miles from the discharge of the Elk River. They named the post Chipewyan, because it was intended particularly for the trade with the Chipewyan. Later, in 1804, traders abandoned this location in favor of the north shore at the western end of Lake Athabasca, where fish were plentiful. Nor'Westers soon called the place "the Athens of the North," not only because of its strategic location but also because of its library, collected by Roderick and others, which boasted among other works the great picaresque novel of the age, *Tristram Shandy,* some classics, and manuals on navigation.

The first year of operations at Fort Chipewyan showed the wisdom of Alexander Mackenzie's plan. The post enjoyed sufficient supplies, for the nearby Peace River, with its extensive game, was becoming both the larder of the northern trade and the greatest source of furs for Fort Chipewyan. Formerly, the Chipewyan had made a seven-month journey to the Bay; now, coming to the principal post in Athabasca, they seemed agreeable to the new arrangements. Mackenzie offered them large credits, which they promised to repay in due time. For the moment, however, Mackenzie could place no reliance on Chipewyan coming to the post; such regularity of trade would have to develop over time. As for the Cree in that area, not only were they few in number, but also, as Mackenzie moaned, they had "done little or nothing these three years. They are always in the same place close by the fort and they have ruined it." Mackenzie intended to relocate the Cree, which he did by giving them goods at the River Fish, many miles to the north, where there was plenty of game.

Mackenzie fought to rein in those men of the company who preferred the wandering summer life with the natives, as he thought them a bad influence on business and other employees. He regarded the tendency of his traders to "go native," and to become bushrangers along the former lines of the *coureurs de bois,* as contrary to strict management of business affairs. He also instituted economy measures, sending out only as many traders as were needed for the circuit of nearby native groups.

By late summer, with his affairs attended to as much as possible, Mackenzie packed for his voyage to the Pacific. Unalaska or Kodiak must have seemed a long way away to him and to those he convinced to accompany him. Who knew if any of them would return? But such thoughts are not for the adventurous, and Mackenzie set them aside to pursue a route across the continent and the discovery of a northwest passage.

CHAPTER 4

The Quest: To the Arctic

DEH-CHO, "the River Big," is what the Dene call the huge stream that drains their homeland Denendeh. The Mackenzie River, what the early explorers called the Great River of the North, courses through northwestern Canada for 2,635 miles. It rises in the Rocky Mountains, flows south, east, and north via the Peace and its tributaries. Then, gathering together the waters of the immense Athabasca, Great Slave, and Great Bear Lakes, it drains into the Arctic Ocean and Beaufort Sea. The Finlay and Parsnip join to form the Peace River, and the Slave River flows to Great Slave Lake. Altogether they form a vast upper river watershed leading to Great Slave Lake. And it is from Great Slave Lake that the Mackenzie River becomes the proper flume leading northward, 1,120 miles to saltwater at Mackenzie Bay.

This upper maze was known to Alexander Mackenzie and fellow traders only by Indian report. What was not known was the course of this immense river. Mackenzie discovered a river nowhere less than half a mile wide, and often three or four miles in width along its lower reaches. Its course lay through virgin wilderness, wooded along its banks all the way to the ocean. The Great River of the North, we now know, cuts through lands rich in minerals, petroleum, and natural gas.

Before Mackenzie's time this vast watershed of spectacular scenery and abundant wildlife was unknown to Europeans. Such nonnative outsiders could only imagine its existence.

The natives knew its secrets, and they liked to joke about the intruding "discoverers." "Alexander Mackenzie came to our land," remarked Dene historian and politician Stephen Kakfwi two centuries later. "He described us in his Journal as a 'meagre, ill-made people . . . people with scabby legs.' " Kakfwi pondered what the Dene thought of Mackenzie: "My people probably wondered at this strange, pale man in his ridiculous clothes, asking about some great waters he was searching for. He recorded his views on the people, but we'll never know exactly how my people saw him. I know they'd never understand why their river is named after such an insignificant fellow."

The Dene continued to call their river Deh-Cho, or Decho, in defiance of the official name as adopted by Canada. In its own way this difference represents the duality of historical understanding of contact and of occupation. On the one hand, Mackenzie may have been derisive, as Kakfwi suggests, in his remarks on the Dene. On the other hand, in its own way, Kakfwi's remark belittles Mackenzie's own achievement, seeking as it does to portray him as a ridiculous stranger lost in Denendeh, the Dene homeland. Mackenzie himself never doubted his dependence on natives. His journeys across northwestern Canada depended on knowledge that he could gain only from natives. When such information was not available, however, as happened from time to time, he went on alone. He was not always on a guided tour.

At nine o'clock in the morning of Wednesday, 3 June 1789, Mackenzie and his party embarked at Fort Chipewyan destined for parts unknown. There was likely still plenty of ice on Great Slave Lake, but they had left as early as the breakup of ice would allow. Their goal was the Pacific Ocean. Mackenzie was in one canoe, Mr. Laurent Leroux, a company clerk, in another. The two men represented a powerful combination.

Leroux, a dynamic figure in commercial expansion in

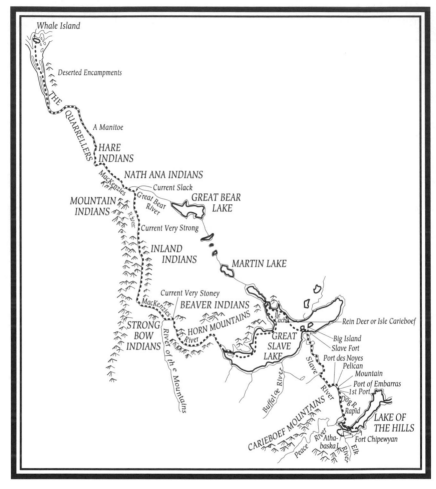

Whale Island

Deserted Encampments

THE QUARRELLERS

A Manitoe

HARE INDIANS

NATH ANA INDIANS

Current Slack

MOUNTAIN INDIANS

Mackenzies River

Great Bear River

GREAT BEAR LAKE

Current Very Strong

INLAND INDIANS

MARTIN LAKE

Current Very Stoney

Mackenzies River

BEAVER INDIANS

STRONG BOW INDIANS

HORN MOUNTAINS

Ile à la Cache

GREAT SLAVE LAKE

Rein Deer or Isle Carieboef

Big Island

Slave Fort

River of the Mountains

Buffaloe River

Slave River

Port des Noyes

Pelican Mountain

Port of Embarras

1st Port

Dog R.

Rapid

CARIEBOEF MOUNTAINS

Peace River

Atha-baska I.

Elk River

LAKE OF THE HILLS

Fort Chipewyan

2. Mackenzie's journey from Fort Chipewyan to the Arctic Ocean. Adapted from the 1801 edition of Mackenzie's *Voyages from Montreal*, with original spellings of place-names.

Athabasca, was bound first for Great Slave Lake. The self-centered Mackenzie gives scant mention of his fellow trader. We learn from other sources that three years earlier, in 1786, Leroux and his men had constructed a small post for the concern on Great Slave Lake. Four years older than Mackenzie, Leroux also came from a military family; his father had been in the Canadian service of the king of France. Quebec-born Leroux, like Mackenzie, had become a bookkeeper before entering Gregory, McLeod and Company. Just as Mackenzie had been deployed to Detroit, Leroux had been dispatched to Michilimackinac. In 1786 he had been sent to Great Slave Lake to counter the opposition being raised from the North West Company under Cuthbert Grant. The competition grew cutthroat and violent, someone took Ross's life, and Gregory, McLeod and Company amalgamated in the summer of 1786 to end the struggle.

In Leroux's keeping was the firm's most northwesterly trade. That summer of 1789 saw the Nor'Westers consolidating and making a profit in the waterways and lands near Fort Chipewyan. From his base at Fort Providence, or Old Fort Providence, on Yellowknife Bay on Great Slave Lake, Leroux could conduct business in a more northwesterly route than the Mackenzie River allowed, that is, toward La Martre Lake. Leroux's plan for 1789 called for him to expand that trade and then retrace his route to a prearranged rendezvous with Mackenzie. The plan was successfully completed, and both men pursued complementary missions of discovery and trade that season. Their lives show interesting parallels. Not only were they both important explorers—Leroux was the first European to explore Great Slave Lake—but also both retired as prosperous merchant traders and became members of the same Lower Canada legislative assembly.

Mackenzie's "crew" consisted of four Canadian men, two of whom were accompanied by their wives. There was also a German, John Steinbruck, whose appearance in Athabasca remains a mystery. The four Canadians were Joseph Landry and Charles Ducette, destined to go a few years later on the renewed Pacific quest, François Barrieau, and Pierre de Lorme. Two small canoes completed the flotilla. One contained the native who had acquired the title of the English Chief, or Nestabeck as Mackenzie also called him, with his two wives and two younger Indian men. The other canoe contained his followers. "These men were engaged to serve us in the twofold capacity of interpreters and hunters," Mackenzie wrote in his Journal for that first day. As for the English Chief, follower of the equally famed Matonabbee, Samuel Hearne's guide in his expedition to the Coppermine River, Mackenzie described him as "a principal leader of his countrymen who were in the habit of carrying furs to [the Hudson's Bay Company's] Churchill Factory . . . and till of late very much attached to the interest of that company. These circumstances procured for him the appelation of the English Chief." Yet another canoe carried articles of trade and was under the charge of Leroux. "In this," explained Mackenzie in his *Voyages,*

> I was obliged to ship part of our provision; which, with the clothing necessary for us on the voyage, a proper assortment of the articles of merchandise as presents, to ensure us a friendly reception among the Indians, and the ammunition and arms requisite for defence, as well as a supply for our hunters, were more than our own canoe could carry, but by the time we should part company, there was every reason to suppose that our expenditure would make sufficient room for the whole.

The expedition had an auspicious start in fine weather. By seven in the evening, when they rested their paddles and made camp on the banks of Slave River, thirty-eight miles of lake and river route lay behind them. Here the hunters began their work, killing a goose and a pair of ducks. As elsewhere on occasion, the men took the canoe out of the

water to regum its seams. The party was once more afloat
on their river journey at four in the morning, soon shooting
the first rapids. Later, at Dog River, near Fitzgerald (formerly Smith's Landing), they camped for the second night,
close to the rapids that would present them with early-
morning labor at sunrise.

On the third day, 5 June, the backbreaking toil began
early and continued late: the portages, both numerous and
long, were made more difficult by ice, driftwood, steep
landing places, and violent currents. The party lost an Indian
canoe down the falls with its "menage," though the Indian
women fortunately jumped to shore in safety. In 1786 those
same river rapids had claimed two canoes and five men under
charge of Cuthbert Grant the Elder, working for Pond in
opposition to Gregory, McLeod and Company. The evening
meal and bed must have come none too early. Mackenzie,
who had a reputation for driving his party, records nothing
of how he himself felt, stating only, "Men and Indians
much fatigued."

Next morning brought speedy travel on the river and
comparative easy going. Then a cold wind set in strongly,
right against their course. A storm brought on a downpour.
The canoe had to be unloaded to prevent the contents from
getting wet. Again on 8 June it "blew exceeding hard with
rain all last Night." No attempt was made to stir from camp.
In succeeding days mosquitoes became troublesome, and
so did the ice that covered their fishing nets. Hunters went
out from time to time from their camps and returned with
geese, duck, swan, and beaver. By day the paddlers worked
through seas of broken ice, worried that their frail birch-
bark canoes would be slashed and filled with water. They
mended canoes as required, and while on shore they gathered cranberries and spring onions. The daylight grew in
length, until at eleven in the evening the explorer could still
put pen to paper and record his observations.

On 23 June the party landed at some lodges of the Yellow-knives, or Redknifes as Mackenzie called them, whose blades were fashioned from copper. These people had promised faith and friendship to Leroux. The Yellowknives said that others of their tribe, plus some Slaves and Beavers, would be there soon, "by the time that the Swans cast their feathers." The English Chief now featured in the diplomacy, for having many old credits in the country he began calling in past debts. To pay off his own debts and to buy a few necessaries and some rum, the English Chief, in turn, gave the furs to Leroux. These preliminaries gave promise of a permanent trade with these people. Mackenzie called all the natives together and told them that he would leave Leroux behind to complete the trading and that he intended to build a post there for as long as they would bring skins enough and "as long as they would deserve it." The natives replied that having traders among them would be "great encouragement" for them, that they would work hard to kill beaver for good value, and that this would give them means of checking the Chipewyan, who always robbed them and thus destroyed their initiative in hunting beaver.

Soon it was time for Leroux to take his departure from the exploring expedition. He cached two bags of pemmican on an island to await his return. Then, on 25 June, he struck out north and west for the trading ground, apparently a little more assured than Mackenzie was about his where-abouts and destination. Leroux's men saluted Mackenzie with several volleys, and in the gathering quietness the two parties made their separate departures.

At this stage, in late June, Mackenzie's Journal speaks of his being lost in a maze of bays, ice, rocks, and trees. The voyageurs picked their way through a field of broken ice. The exit from Great Slave Lake proved elusive. When the clouds dispersed Mackenzie could get a better indication of his actual position, or astronomical location, by navigational instruments. He could fix his latitude on his map by observing the sun at high noon, and by using his tables, or nautical almanac, he could obtain his approximate longitude. Determining his location was easier than finding his way. On many occasions he could not find his passage out of labyrinthine bays and waters. He had to fall back on native knowledge, and often this was incomplete or even faulty. Mackenzie consulted with local people on several occasions. He pressed them to reveal geographical secrets, but drew a blank. "They know nothing even of the [Mackenzie] River but [only] the Entry," he complained. He paid a young man to escort the expedition in order to avoid "circumnavigating bays." For the short term, such advice could speed up the expedition, and that was Mackenzie's immediate aim.

They pressed on, entering a markedly different terrain—one of barren headlands, islands, and stunted trees. It was, the explorer noted, one continuous view of mountains, islands, and solid rock. They completed the traverse of the lake at last. They chanced upon an abandoned Slave camp, a former fishery where the Slaves had kept a rendezvous until the Cree attacked and drove them away, more than ten years before, according to Mackenzie's reckoning by dating some cut trees.

Mackenzie and his party were not out of trouble and often seemed lost. If not tormented by mosquitoes, they were shrouded in fog or surrounded by fields of broken ice. "Our guides [are] quite at a loss," wrote Mackenzie in his Journal with a touch of anger mixed with anxiety. "They do not know what course to take." Eight years had passed since his guide had been in that spot, and one great bay looked very much like the entrance to the river. They hunted in vain, and the English Chief became furious with Redknife for guiding them on a route he did not know. The English Chief was "in a great passion," said Mackenzie, and wanted to shoot the Redknife guide. Mackenzie was angry too, but he intervened on the grounds that certain signs indicated they were "close by the River."

Indeed they were, for rounding a point early the next day, 29 June, they happened upon the passage they had been seeking. They entered on a broad but shallow river, highly banked and treed. It is shown on the first native map of Tutcho (Great Slave Lake) and was known anciently to the Cree as Kis-Ca-Che-Wan, "Swiftly Flowing Waters." Here Mackenzie's real discoveries began. The men raised sail or paddled as required and soon were beyond where the Redknife had ever traveled. They made camp somewhere downstream from where Fort Providence is now situated. Gradually the river, wide and chock-full of islands for a short stretch of ten or fifteen miles, turned more toward the north, and for a time it narrowed. Mackenzie sounded for the river bottom wherever he could, using a lead on a line. This method could last only so long as the lead and line did not get snagged on the bottom. Unfortunately, the line soon got snagged and could not be saved. The party drifted and paddled on, were deluged by a passing rainstorm, and landed and cached two bags of pemmican for future use.

Various rivers joined the Mackenzie, including the muddy waters of what Mackenzie called the River of the Mountain, now the Liard (where the Nor'Westers put up a post at "The Forks" in 1803). He knew that a great river had joined the main stream, for instead of being limpid and clear, the water had become dark and muddy. But Mackenzie and his party never saw the tributary, for the landscape of the morning was shrouded in fog.

On 2 July at mid-morning they saw high hills or mountains stretching as far to the south as the eye could see. At noon they came abreast of the mountains, whose summits looked barren and rocky. The natives pointed out the bright white stones on the top of one of them, which they said were spirit stones, *Manatee aseniah*. Mackenzie at first thought it might be talc, then concluded it was snow in patches. Soon all the members of the party imagined they heard the roar of approaching rapids, but, Mackenzie said, the sound "only subsisted in our imaginations." The next evening, hoping to get a better view, Mackenzie climbed a hill, dubbed later by travelers La Roche Qui Trempe à l'Eau, "the Rock by the Riverside." The results were disappointing, for the countryside was surrounded by hills. To his surprise, however, Mackenzie found a campment on top of the hill— a place where his native friends and their allies could when necessary take refuge against the dreaded Cree. Back on the river after a wearisome, time-consuming climb, Mackenzie and his party surged forth on what now seemed to be a hissing, boiling stream. The weather turned cold, and ice formed at night on the still waters at the edges of the great flume.

And so the days passed. Ever northward the exploring party worked, as current and ice would allow. On 5 July the river widened and the current slackened a little. Their course was now northwesterly, but, alarmingly, a ridge of high, snowy mountains rose ahead of them. Mackenzie said nothing of his fears at that moment. But where did the river wind? It could not traverse those snowclad heights. He was hungry for information. What did the natives know, and where were they? All lay silent along the wilderness waterway.

In the evening, Mackenzie's party spied several smoky fires, and the canoemen paddled toward them as fast as they could. They had chanced on a cluster of Slave and Dogrib families in their camp. These people were Northern Athabaskans, hunters and fishers, and at this time they were living unarmed in isolation and fear. They were surprised and frightened when Mackenzie's canoes came into view, and took to their canoes or to the woods. Not all were swift enough to make the escape, and the fleet-footed native hunters in the explorer's party were able to track some of them down. The hunters spoke to the Slave and Dogrib in the Chipewyan language, which at first they seemed not to comprehend—only using signs to warn off the intruders. Meanwhile, Mackenzie and his party made camp, pitched tents, and unloaded their goods and gifts. The English Chief and his young men became artful diplomats at this stage, reconciling these Slave and Dogrib to the arrival of the exploring party. "When their Flurry was over," recorded Mackenzie, "and they saw we intended them no hurt, it was found that some of the Men understood our Indians very well, who persuaded them to come down to where we were which they consented to with great Reluctance, and not without evident signs of Fear, but the Reception they met with partly removed their Terror, and they recalled the rest of their People from their hiding Places."

It was a meeting of strangers, and precautions were necessarily taken. The traders had kept their distance, at the demands of those whose seclusion had been violated. Once the English Chief and his young men had convinced the Slave and Dogrib that Mackenzie and party meant no one any harm, the traders doled out tokens of friendship: ironware, trinkets, rum, and tobacco. Soon the Indians became too familiar, and it was difficult for the traders to keep them out of their tents. But they did not steal or try to steal, as far as the cautious Mackenzie could observe. They had a ready knowledge of the manufactured items and other trade goods, but tobacco and alcoholic beverages were new to them. "We made them smoke," recounted Mackenzie, "tho' it was evident they did not know the use of Tobacco. We likewise gave them some grog to drink, but I believe they accepted those Civilities more through Fear than Inclination."

Mackenzie traded for beaver and marten, but his mind soon turned to the river's course. He interrogated the Slave and Dogrib, hoping for some scrap of information that would lead him to his hoped-for destination, but he was disappointed. He recorded in his Journal:

> The Information they gave us respecting the River, seems to me so very *fabulous* that I will be particular in inserting [it in my account]. Suffice it to say that they would wish to make us believe that we would be several Winters getting to the Sea, and that we all should be old men by the time we would return. That we would have to encounter many Monsters (which can only exist in their own Imaginations). Besides that there are 2 impracticable Falls or Rapids in the River, the first 30 Days March from us.

Mackenzie put no faith in these accounts, but the English Chief and his young men, already tired from exertions, had quite a different reaction. They concluded, and demanded, that the explorer should quit, and that they all should return immediately to Fort Chipewyan. They feared starvation in a land where few animals were thought to exist. The farther they went, they argued, the hungrier they would become. Again Mackenzie's diplomacy, even bribery, was effective. "I with much ado dissuaded them out of their Reasonings," he recounted of his palaver with the English Chief and his men, "and made them to ask one of the Natives to accompany us, which they soon did." The new recruit, as Mackenzie called him, had no great desire to undertake the mission and had to be forced to embark. After taking note of the features and dancing of the Slave and Dogrib—important ethnographic data in its own right—Mackenzie returned to his canoe and to the challenge. He left behind acquaintances willing to await his return from his voyage. Before nightfall they were beyond the entrance to Great Bear River, which carries clear green water from that largest of northern lakes, Great Bear Lake. Along the way "our new conductor," also called "our stranger," gave information of a land populous in bear and small white buffalo in the mountains (that is, mountain goats and sheep). The ridge of snowy mountains always stood in sight toward the setting sun. Mackenzie yearned for a view from a hilltop—but even then, when a high rocky hill presented itself, his design was thwarted by swarms of mosquitoes.

On 7 July Mackenzie took the cautious route as advised by the Redknife. The party was now at the Sans Sault Rapids, the most difficult, dangerous stretch of the river to canoe. Following the recommendation of the guide, they portaged. Then they found that the stream would have been quite navigable. With a heavy dose of sarcasm Mackenzie wrote, "This proved to be one of the dangerous Rapids we had to pass & convinced me in my Opinion respecting the falsity of the Natives Information." At this juncture some of the natives ran away, leaving only Mackenzie's Redknife guide, whom Mackenzie styled "Our Conductor," and an old man and old woman. The English Chief and his entourage remained with Mackenzie. Apparently those natives who had run away could be brought back at the whim of the old man, who called for presents. Mackenzie brought forth the requisite articles—knives, beads, awls, and the like—and soon the natives were pacified and pleased.

The conductor wanted to quit the enterprise. Mackenzie, by means not stated, forced him to embark and to continue. Four canoes followed Mackenzie's, altogether forming a small flotilla. Mackenzie, alert to dangers of the stream, posted one of his traders or voyageurs in each of the native canoes to make sure that the portage around the next, promised rapids would be found. "They like the other people told us many discouraging Stories," he recounted of his recent informants. These natives, it seems, had underestimated the abilities and the daring of the Canadian voyageurs. In the end, however, the canoes passed safely down the narrow channel.

Late that evening Mackenzie received his first warning of the Eskimo or, as they call themselves in Canada, the Inuit, "the people." Nowadays they are styled the Mackenzie Inuit, or Inuvialuit, the western Arctic Inuit of the Mackenzie River. In Mackenzie's time they lived in numerous local groups, always changing, that fringed Arctic waters from Greenland to Siberia. Migratory hunters, they roamed the lower Mackenzie River area and were few in number. They traded with the Dene and other natives, bringing iron for making knives. They had a reputation for violence. One of Mackenzie's hunters described them not only as "very wicked" but also as very likely to murder Mackenzie's men. Two summers before, it seems, a great party of Inuit had come far up the river and killed some of the informant's relatives. Mackenzie learned of violent struggles between Dene and Inuit.

Now another crisis came upon them, for the conductor again wished to abandon the enterprise. "Our Conductor," recorded Mackenzie on 9 July, "like the others wanted to leave us here. He was afraid that we should not come back this way, & besides that the Eskmeaux would perhaps kill us & take their Women from my Men & Indians, & that he was afraid of them too." The natives with Mackenzie brazenly told the conductor that they were not afraid and that he ought not to be either. Certainly they would all return by this way. The conductor embarked, and the canoe pushed off. Mackenzie pondered this new information: "Those Indians told me that from where I met the first of their People this Morning it was not far to go to the Sea over Land on the East Side & from where I found them it was but a short way to go to it to the Westwd. that the land on both sides the River was like a Point." Mackenzie noted these particulars dutifully in his Journal, but did not comment. In an unknown country—even lost—Mackenzie had no geographical basis to challenge his informants.

The party had now traveled down and through the Ramparts—that grand scenic wonder of the river where the majestic waterway, mile-wide, rushes through a gorge three to four hundred feet wide. Beyond the Lower Ramparts, on 10 July, Mackenzie observed differences in the environment. The snowy mountains, the Rockies, lay ten miles away to the west. The river had widened and now ran in many channels among countless islands. There were larger trees than any they had seen in the past ten days. Ice lay on the banks above the river, left there by the rapidly falling stream.

Mackenzie took an observation at noon (67°47′ north latitude) and added laconically to his Journal that this was "further North than I expected, according to the course I kept, but the difference is partly owing to the variation of the Compass which is more Easterly than that I thought." And, indeed, the farther north he traveled, the greater the magnetic variation became. He was in a land of endless day, and nights became full daylight hours. Mackenzie could sit up and watch the curious passage of the sun in those latitudes.

But where was he? Mackenzie was at a loss as to his location and admitted as much in his Journal. He knew that Pond's entry to the Pacific did not lie in this direction. He was certain that going farther north on the main river channel "will not answer the Purpose of which the Voyage was intended, as it is evident these waters must empty themselves into the Northern Ocean." The conductor groaned at having to go on, claiming that he had never seen the *Benahulla Toe,* "White Man's Lake." Mackenzie believed he could not get back to Fort Chipewyan by the end of the traveling season and decided to go "to the discharge of those waters." His hunters, he wrote, were "quite disquieted with my voyage." Mackenzie told them that he would go on for seven days more, and that if he did not reach the sea in that time, he would begin the return journey. The party continued on, past remnants of Inuit camps, piles of whale bones, and a house for drying fish. The weather grew raw and disagreeable, and the hunters continued to complain. A new realization dawned: that they were near the shores of the Arctic Sea.

On 12 July they paddled to an island, Richard, from which they could see water covered with ice for six miles. This was the limit of their travels. Mackenzie and the English Chief mounted the summit of a hill for a better view. As far as the eye could see, all around lay water and, to the southwest, distant mountains. They pondered this maze of water and land, this complex and baffling delta. Was this the sea? Mackenzie did not think so, or perhaps did not choose to think so. He called it in his Journal "the entrance of the lake." Apparently he clung to the thought that it could not be saltwater. In his Journal he expressed the disappointment they all felt: "My men express much sorrow that they are obliged to return without seeing the Sea; in which I believe them sincere for we marched exceeding hard coming down the River, and I never heard them grumble; but on the contrary in good Spirits, and in hope every day that the next would bring them to the *Mer d'Ouest,* and declare themselves now and at any time ready to go with me whenever I choose to lead them."

They had not reached the western sea. The rising tide that awakened them and the sight of beluga whales sporting in the bay beyond their camp island led Mackenzie to the incontrovertible conclusion that this was the Arctic Sea. Still, he continued his research and tried to find some Inuit who could give him more information about the shoreline. The conductor advised that the Inuit had gone on their annual whaling and caribou-hunting expeditions. Besides, the water had become very deep. Mackenzie decided that the party should return to the river, where they found shelter from the winds but were much tormented by mosquitoes in consequence.

If Mackenzie was disappointed he did not record this in the pages of his Journal. From the search for a western lake he turned his attention to the habitat. He recorded particulars of that place in that time, which are now invaluable for the environmental historian. He made notes on berries, plants, and herbs; on wildlife, especially birds; and on rock, sand, and clay, particularly red earth "which the Natives bedaub themselves with." Aware that many contemporary European intellectuals were curious about the botany and zoology of the globe, Mackenzie took pains to portray a new and uncharted world for science, one now known to be a fragile ecosystem. Of permafrost, he wrote: "I had my Hanger in my Hand & tried frequently in any part of the ground thaw'd but cou'd never make it enter above 6 or 8 inches."

On 14 July—precisely the same day when an angry Paris mob was storming that ancient prison-fortress the Bastille and ushering in the French Revolution—Mackenzie was making a testament to his northernmost thrust. That morning he fixed a post on Whale Island, "on which I engraved the latitude of the place, my own name, the number of persons I had with me, and the time we had been here." Whale Island's location has been a subject of controversy, but Garry Island resembles Mackenzie's bivouac in size and shape. No record exists that the post, planted close by Mackenzie's camp, has ever been found by Europeans.

Mackenzie now began the upriver journey, against a very strong current. The passage was tedious and the work laborious. The Redknife guide took his leave, totally unannounced. Apparently frightened that Mackenzie intended to make him a slave, and perhaps to kill him, he vanished, leaving behind a shirt that Mackenzie had given him, so that he would not be in debt to the explorer.

By 27 July they were well on their way upriver, and from Dene people Mackenzie learned that the natives knew of no river of the West except by hearsay. They claimed that none of them had gone beyond the western mountains. There was talk, however, of a river that led toward the midday sun. From one Dene he learned of a European-style fort and concluded: "this I take to be Unalaschka Fort & of course the River to the west to be Cooks River & this to fall into or join with Noxta [Norton] Sound not as a River but a body of dead water." Mackenzie could not get a guide to go westward with him. Presents and bribes would not work. The natives told fascinating and fabulous accounts of the people beyond the mountains—"that the People at the Entry of the River kill men with their Eyes"—and Mackenzie found himself at a loss as to how to get accurate information. Yet he was not resigned to his circumstances, even though he had apparently exhausted the patience of his guides. "It is very certain that those People know more about the Country than they chuse to tell me at least than what comes to my Ears," he wrote. "I am obliged to depend upon my Interpreter for all News, his being now & long since tired of the Voyage may occasion him to conceal from me part of what the Natives tell him for fear he should be obliged to undergo more fatigues—tho' he has always declared to me that he would not abandon me wherever I went." Mackenzie made one last, desperate attempt to get at the truth; he needed guides, and offered iron and beads for their pains. Despite his feigned appearance of anger, he got nowhere. Exploration westward would have to await another season. They passed by "oil seeps," where oil was discovered nearly a century and a half later, in 1925, and they saw a seam of burning lignite, still burning in our own times.

By 22 August they had reached the entrance of Great Slave Lake, where they made sail as much as heavy winds would allow. On the next day:

> We paddled a long way into a deep Bay to take the wind, when we came to hoist sail, we found we had forgotten our Mast at our Campment, landed and cut another, hoisted half sail which drove us on at a great rate, at 12 the wind and swell augmented much, our underyard broke, but luckily our Mast Top resisted till we had time to fasten down the Yard with a Pole without lowering sail, took in much water, and had our Mast given way in all probability we should have filled and sunk.

These freshwater argonauts sailed heavy seas, and they went on in great danger along a nasty lee shore. Two men bailed frantically as water came in on every side, until at last the canoe doubled a point that provided a screen from the wind and swell. There the party camped, gummed the canoe, set their nets, and waited out the storm.

The next day, 24 August, Mackenzie and his men were reunited with Leroux's advance guard, returning from their enterprise. The trade had not met expectations, for the natives were afraid of the Europeans and needed material inducements to trade. Leroux at last arrived, but the English Chief defected for a time. Mackenzie now ordered Leroux to stay behind and carry on the winter trade. Mackenzie also ordered the English Chief to trade in the land of the Beaver Indians and to bring their beaver and marten to Leroux and to Athabasca next March. These arrangements complete, on 1 September in fine calm weather Mackenzie was again in his canoe, passing the Isle la Cache where several months earlier provisions had been secreted for Leroux. Overhead, numerous flocks of wildfowl headed southward. It rained in streams; the canoe broke during a portage, forcing a delay for repairs; the men were much fatigued.

Friday the 11th of September was the next to last day of

this adventure. The men were up early, at four, and trod the frozen ground. There was an appearance of snow, they took to the water, and they made an early camp. The next day, with a wind from the northeast, they entered Lake Athabasca. They were not far from their return destination. "The Wind veered to the Westward, and as strong as we could bear it with high Sail, which wafted us to Fort Chipewean."

Upon his return to Fort Chipewyan, 102 days after setting out, Mackenzie had completed a round trip of nearly 3,000 miles. His cousin Roderick observed that the perilous undertaking had been experienced without any material accident. This was a remarkable feat, and the fact that the various natives knew of these waters, or segments of them, should not deny the significance of the wayfarer coursing through what was to the wider world unknown territory.

Had Mackenzie not kept his Journal of this voyage, in which he recorded the events of the journey for posterity, modern understanding of the opening of the Northwest would have been lessened. In an era that disparages heroes, Mackenzie's northern achievement remains a mighty contribution to the empirical comprehension of the vast landscape. This success can never be taken away from him. In fact, these on-the-ground gatherings of data are little more than Mackenzie claimed for himself. He never pretended to have found a northwest passage, or to have gone beyond Samuel Hearne's achievements of being the first European to stand on the Arctic shores of America or of proving the nonexistence of a water throughway across the continent. The exploration and discovery of the Mackenzie River formed a distinct step in the exploration of the Canadian North, especially the sub-Arctic. It opened to fur traders an access to present-day Mackenzie District and Yukon Territory. The map of the far Northwest—including the northern interior of British Columbia, the western Northwest Territories, the

Yukon, and eastern Alaska—was expanded by Mackenzie's energies. For a century and more, successors of Mackenzie and Leroux pushed their trade into every creek and valley. They continued the exploration of this vast quarter of the continent and opened the Yukon before the discovery of gold. Erecting posts on lakes and rivers, they set up a network of trade with the natives long before missionaries arrived to plant the cross or government agents came to raise the flag. Mackenzie's exploration, we now know, served an additional purpose, that of giving explorers an important access to the Arctic. The Mackenzie River was used thus by John Franklin in 1820, and in later years this British naval officer explored much of the north coast of mainland North America from the delta of the Mackenzie River.

Thirty-five years after Mackenzie stood at the Arctic shoreline, Franklin, who possessed vastly superior instruments, confirmed the accuracy of his predecessor's observations. "The survey of the Mackenzie made on this Expedition differs very little in its outline from that of its discoverer, whose general correctness we had often occasion to admire." The compliment was handsome, and it came from an explorer who had made good use of advice from Mackenzie. Admittedly, differences existed on several points of latitude. Franklin attributed these errors to the fact that Mackenzie had laid down latitudes by compass bearings and to his lack of means of detecting changes in magnetic variation, which are wild in that region. Mackenzie's northern legacy was assured: The mouth of the Mackenzie River had been fixed correctly on the chart and the general course of the river delineated. Franklin's testimonial speaks volumes.

Mackenzie may have named the great waterway, as he called it on one occasion, the "River Disappointment." Certainly it was that to him. He also referred to it as the Grand River, a name that is nearly identical to the Dene appellation Deh-Cho, "the River Big." Mackenzie and Leroux pushed the fur trade throughout its headwaters in subsequent seasons. They commenced the development of the river as a highway of opportunity. Within a century paddle-wheel steamers plied the lakes and rivers of the Mackenzie River system, and a series of communities were linked by steam and by telegraph.

Of Laurent Leroux's preliminary contributions to this northwestern enterprise it may be noted that he put up a post, Fort Providence, on Great Slave Lake. Then he traded at one time or another with the Slave, Beaver, and Chipewyan natives. He was followed on the Mackenzie River proper by Duncan Livingston, who built a Canadian establishment ninety miles downstream from Great Slave Lake. In 1799 Livingston and four of his party were killed, either by Inuit or by their native guides, in the course of an exploratory march downstream from the post. The next year the Nor'Wester John Thompson, Livingston's successor, diverted the trade to Great Bear Lake and to Rocky Mountain House. For a long period thereafter the Mackenzie River itself saw few trading posts erected on its banks, while many were closed in the Hudson's Bay Company consolidation of the 1820s.

To return to Mackenzie, in mid-June 1790 he made his way out to the annual rendezvous at Grand Portage, along with Patrick Small from Ile-à-la-Crosse, Angus Shaw from Moose Lake, and William McGillivray, the latter soon to be a rising star in the Nor'Westers' management. Mackenzie's fellow travelers recognized his northern achievement, and when they came upon a fine sturgeon fishery, they toasted him with "eggnogs," sturgeon roe stirred briskly while pouring in the rum.

The party reached Cumberland House, where they were greeted by Hudson's Bay Company men, including the surveyor Philip Turnor and Peter Fidler, his apprentice. At seven in the evening, recorded Turnor, "Mr Alex Mackenzie the Master of the Athapiscow Lake settlement and its dependencies arrived with one Canoe in which he had 20 Packs of furs besides his own things which is not common for a Canadian Master to have as they mostly keep their own Canoe for their own things." The Cumberland House journal observed that

> Messrs Small, McKenzie, Shaw and McGillivray Masters of the Canadian Settlements to the Northwest, arrived in their passage out. They informed me that they had had a good winter both with respect to Trade and Provisions. Mr. McKenzie says that he has been to the Sea, but thinks it the Hyperborean [Northern] Sea but he does not seem acquainted with Observations which makes me think he is not well convinced where he has been.

So wrote Turnor, himself about to set off on his own survey of the Athabasca Lake region. The Bay traders, playing catch-up, had instructed Turnor and several assistants to explore and map the far western waterways. The lands south and west of Hearne's discoveries to the mouth of the Coppermine River remained unknown to them. The Hudson's Bay Company knew of Pond's post near Lake Athabasca and could only imagine his further intentions, with which Mackenzie was familiar. Turnor disparaged Mackenzie's scientific abilities, and Mackenzie was well aware of his own deficiencies in this regard. Turnor, according to the great mapmaker David Thompson, was a man well versed in mathematics, a compiler of nautical almanacs, and a practical astronomer—high praise from such a source. Turnor and Mackenzie exchanged views on surveying and exploration.

Mackenzie had his own opinions on all of this. He wrote to his cousin Roderick at Fort Chipewyan that apparently Turnor was merely exploring and that for the time being he was not going to Lake Athabasca to trade, so that Roderick could extend hospitality to him without fear of competition. Of his meeting with Turnor, confided Alexander, "I find the intention [of the expedition] is only discoveries. I also find the party is very ill prepared for their undertaking." Fidler, accompanying Malchom Ross, Turnor, and their party, left Cumberland House on 13 September bound on a mission whose aim the young man understood as follows: "Our sole motive for going to the Athapescow is for Mr. Turnor to survey these parts in order to settle some dubious points." Hearne and Pond, remarked Fidler, had fixed these places on their maps farther to the west than good reason would allow.

The effect on Mackenzie of this encounter with a well-trained and agreeable man of science like Turnor is not known. He was already well aware of those defects in his navigational abilities and chart making. Turnor, on the other hand, knew exactly where he was in terms of astronomical observations, and he gave Mackenzie a much-needed lesson. Mackenzie decided to spend a winter in England mastering the art. Like Pond, Mackenzie had insufficient knowledge of astronomy and of the making of accurate observations. Pond, said Judge Ogden, was equipped with instruments, but he lacked scientific training. The scientific world in London, so intimately connected to the Hudson's Bay Company, the East India Company, the Admiralty, War Office, and Royal Society, frowned on anything that could not be documented. Science was king. In the same year of 1790 Dalrymple reported glowingly of Turnor's prospects and disparaged Pond: "Discoverers would profit by the information of Mr Turnor, whom the Hudson's Bay Company had sent into those parts, and from whose Astronomical abilities we may reasonably expect competent Information, whereas Peter Pond's allegation . . . betrays his *ignorance* or impudence and invalidates any Reports coming from him."

Those who have studied voyage literature and have noted discrepancies in the reading of longitude specifically will realize that even the most highly trained and practiced users of instruments did not always reach the hoped-for precision of measurement. Reading the narratives and charts of Captains James Cook, George Vancouver, and F. W. Beechey shows that accuracy was approximate, not absolute. As regards latitude, Mackenzie's observations made on the Mackenzie River on 24 June 1789 were about seven miles out. Mackenzie himself realized he needed more accurate methods, and admitted as much. He recalled later that "in this voyage [to the Arctic], I was not only without the necessary books and instruments, but also felt myself deficient in the sciences of astronomy and navigation. I did not hesitate therefore to undertake a winter's voyage in order to procure the one and acquire the other."

At least one other reason compelled Mackenzie toward spending some time in London. "My *Expedition* was hardly spoken of, but that is what I expected," wrote Mackenzie acidly to Roderick from Grand Portage on 16 July 1790. He felt isolated and dejected. He received little news of family and friends. "Every body had plenty of Letters and news from Montreal except myself," he complained. Attending the gathering of partners there, Mackenzie heard little that was gratifying. Simon McTavish, sarcastically nicknamed Le Marquis, haughtily complained that the Athabasca region was sending down too few furs. McTavish delighted in putting the knife in and turning it, too. Mackenzie's temper simmered at this time, and rose again closer to the boil. And although Mackenzie was not alone in his hatred of the domineering Nor'Wester overlord, other partners expressed no great enthusiasm for further explorations in that quarter. Jealous or envious of Mackenzie's northern achievement, they made no acknowledgment of its value or even novelty—none at least that would satisfy the disgruntled discoverer. Not even the fact that the North West Company partners voted Mackenzie a second share, giving him two shares out of twenty, provided a balm. Thus, when Mackenzie returned to the wilderness for the winter campaign of 1790–91, a new revelation had come to him: achievement in and of itself counted for nothing; recognition of that achievement counted for all.

As this insight dawned on Mackenzie, and as he mulled over new stratagems, he worked at reorganizing the trade at Fort Chipewyan. He placed his cousin Roderick at the mouth of the Yellowknife River. He completed his Canadian correspondence and then embarked for England. In Quebec, Mackenzie's partner Frobisher wrote to Simon McGillivray in London to say that McGillivray would be surprised to know that Mackenzie has "taken his passage & is gone Home." Mackenzie had told Frobisher of his surprise that McTavish had made a secret deal with Gregory behind his back. Mackenzie and his associate Daniel Sutherland "seem to be in the Dumps about it, tho' they never hinted the least thing to me."

Mackenzie plotted revenge. He and others saw McTavish's arrangements as fixed, binding, inflexible. The interior traders, who lobbied Mackenzie at this time, worried that the Detroit and Michilimackinac trades were slipping into the hands of American rivals. They looked to establish a new company to carry on the trade in Lake Superior and the Northwest.

All these matters boiled in Mackenzie's mind that winter in London. He had much to read and to ponder. Those numerous books of travel, of seaborne exploration and trade, and of international rivalry on the northwest coast and the Pacific—by John Meares, Nathaniel Portlock, George Dixon, and others—showed that the Nootka Sound crisis had merely opened the door to British commerce on the far side of America. William Coxe's celebrated *Account of the Russian Discoveries between Asia and America* was then in its third edition and told of Russian eastward progress. Alexander Dalrymple's *Plan for Promoting the Fur-Trade*

*and Securing it to this Country by Uniting the Operations
of the East-India and Hudson's Bay Companys* was also available on the bookstalls. Meares's assertions had been refuted in pamphlets by maritime explorer Dixon. By the time Mackenzie arrived in London, John Cadman Etches, a merchant trader to Nootka and China, had penned a pamphlet entitled *An Authentic Statement of all the Facts Relative to Nootka Sound: Its Discovery, History, Settlement, Trade and Probable Advantages to be Derived from It.* The Americans and the Spanish were already at Nootka Sound. Mackenzie kept his scholarly findings to himself and later mentioned only one such work in his *Voyages from Montreal:* Meares's *Voyages made in the Years 1788 and 1789, from China to the North West Coast of America,* published in November 1790. That trader's inflated speculations about a northwest passage and his report of the American sloop *Lady Washington's* track in 1789 through what is now known to be the Coast Range of British Columbia required closer examination. Meares, a key British government witness in working up the national claims against Spain for trade rights in the Pacific, had many detractors. Mackenzie, if he followed the Dixon-Meares controversy, would have known all the details of this protracted, intricate business.

Mackenzie must have been conversant with the literature of the era on the Pacific. All such information pointed to one fact. No priorities of discovery remained open to him except one: how to get to the northwest coast and the Pacific overland? That was Mackenzie's question. His mind fixed on the Pacific. He attended to the problems of astronomy and navigation. He kept to his obligations of self-improvement. And upon his return to Canada and to the high country he was ready for the final journey.

CHAPTER 5

The Quest: To the Pacific

"I SEND you a couple of Guineas. The rest I take with me to traffick with the Russians. . . . May all happiness attend you, Adieu Dear Roderic. Yours unchangeably, Alexr. McKenzie." When he wrote this flamboyantly from Forks of Peace River on 8 May 1793, the explorer had every intention of reaching the Muscovite posts at Unalaska or Kamchatka. Did he expect to travel overland to St. Petersburg and London? Did he intend to visit Czarina Catherine II at the Winter Palace or even the Hermitage and lay before her the dream of intercontinental commerce across the North Pacific?

The surviving evidence fails to tell us Mackenzie's precise plan. We do know, however, that he was in large measure carrying out a plan developed by Peter Pond. In July 1787 Pond had readied a map and an accompanying letter to be carried by Mackenzie to Pacific shores. He was to present these documents to any Russian fur traders he might meet on the northwest coast, perhaps at Unalaska, so that they could pass them on to their headquarters. Now, five years later, Mackenzie intended to carry out a similar plan, one of his own modification or design.

Mackenzie had no brash intention to forestall the Muscovites trading on the northwest coast. That was out of the question. He knew the Russians were already well planted there, and he hoped only to use them as intermediaries in the grand design of Canadian trade to China.

The great gain to be made by the Canadians would be getting access to the China market by way of the great portal of Kiatka, on the Russian border with northern China. For there, and there only, were caravans permitted to carry furs to Peking and thence to the Celestial Kingdom, which was heavily protected against trade with the *Fan-Kwae*, "foreign devils." At Canton, it is true, the great European maritime nations kept trading-houses, but there the British East India Company exercised sole rights of British trade—rights denied to Canadian traders such as Pond or Mackenzie.

It might be possible to change the nasty octopus of British mercantile regulation that kept the Nor'Westers out of improvements in their trade arrangements—if Mackenzie could open up a commercial link. Only one commercial path led to China from America, and that was the profitable trade in sea otter pelts from the northeastern Pacific. Mackenzie intended to develop this, and now his mind stretched beyond the confines of Athabasca to embrace a larger network. If the geographical hazards ahead of him were formidable, at least the fabulous results would be worth the trouble. Even if he succeeded only in opening up trade with the Russians, he would have mastered the first step of the enterprise. But truly he was making his way in the dark. Without any satisfactory support from the corporation of which he was a partner, yet having its tacit consent, Mackenzie set forth from forks of Peace River on a scheme that was entirely experimental.

Mackenzie knew of recent successes by British pioneers in the sea otter trade with the natives of the northwest coast of North America. In particular, from the findings of Captain Cook's 1778 voyage to Nootka Sound and to "Cook's River," he learned of the seaborne wealth of that region and of the prospects of a trans-Pacific trade to Macao and

Canton. The master mariner had been surprised that the Russians had camped on Alaskan islands. Similarly, Captain Nathaniel Portlock in 1786 at Cook's River (now Cook Inlet) found to his dismay that the Russians had already secured possession of the place before his expedition could do so. Gradually, British traders came to understand that the Russians had carved out an extensive island empire anchored on the eastern reaches of Siberia, at Kamchatka. This trade linkage embraced a whole necklace of islands stretching ever eastward to Kodiak, the Kenai Inlet, Unalaska, and Sitka, or New Archangel. By the time of Mackenzie's death that amazing transoceanic empire, limited only by the problems of supply and foodstuffs, reached south and east to Fort Ross in Alta California, north of San Francisco Bay. Perhaps already the Nor'Westers were too late in their westward progress.

In July 1788 Pond touched up the version of his ever changing map of his discoveries that he intended to give to Empress Catherine. Even then, explorations by British traders, such as John Meares, James Strange, Charles William Barkley, Nathaniel Portlock, George Dixon, and Charles Duncan, were already under way. And who knew what the Bostonians were up to? Fort Chipewyan was far inland. Despite the relative proximity of Athabasca to Nootka Sound—about a thousand miles as the crow flies—all communication had to come from more than half a world away, and then only by way of the vast, forested Canadian wilderness.

Pond and Mackenzie thus had to make their plan in the dark and to garner what scraps of information they could concerning pioneering achievements by sea that were threatening to outflank their interests. By the time Mackenzie set off from Fort Fork on Peace River, the Nootka Sound crisis had blown up between Spain and Britain, and the storm in international affairs had passed. The British, it seems, had intervened in an area where the Spanish had expected only the Russians to be encroaching. Captain Martínez's ill-fated, high-handed seizure of Captain Colnett's vessels at Friendly Cove, Nootka Sound, in 1789 brought a British threat of armed retaliation if the Spanish failed to grant Britain equal access to the trade of the northwest coast, irrespective of the claims of either the British or Spanish empires to territory on that shore. Edmund Burke told the House of Commons that this "distant dominion" ought really to be the sovereign territory of the native peoples, and doubted the wisdom of yet another British annexation in remote parts of the world. But by the resolution of the Nootka crisis, the Spanish admitted that they could not claim universal control over the farthest northwestern extension of New Spain, and they were obliged to share with the British and Russians claims to America in these latitudes. Already the northwest coast lay under three European flags, with the U.S. flag also being shown in various harbors by Bostonians such as Robert Gray and John Kendrick. The Americans were establishing their seaborne commerce that linked eastern ports with Vancouver Island, Alaska, the Hawaiian Islands, Canton, and home again.

What taxed Mackenzie's mind at this juncture was not whether rivals traded on the Pacific Coast but what lay between Fort Chipewyan and the western ocean. No amount of oceanic explorations could unlock such a secret. This affair was his alone. What was the distance between the two points? What waters flowed through the territory? What mountain barriers stood in the way? And what passes offered conduits for future trade and communication? Besides these questions, Mackenzie had to determine what native tribes lived in the areas in between and how they could be brought into the new realm of Canadian-based commerce. He thought nothing at all of the prospects of settlement, which in any case was anathema to the fur trader.

Rather, he saw the far western wilderness as the means to wealth and personal advancement. This all-commanding fixation on exploration was neither altruistic nor self-indulgent but rather hard-headed and practical. Time was now of the essence. Mackenzie had no intention of spending longer in the wilderness than he needed to. His fortune from the fur trade was rising. The passage to the great western sea leading to Asia would soon be found, by some traveler or trader. He and he alone was situated to probe the mountains that separated the northern forest from the western ocean. Mackenzie hurried the plans for his "Journey to the Western Ocean." During the fall of 1792 he drew fresh supplies from the storehouses at Fort Chipewyan. He made his final arrangements and put his books in order.

On 10 October 1792 Mackenzie departed Fort Chipewyan, leaving it under control of the trusty Roderick. "I had resolved to go as far as our most distant settlement, which would occupy the remaining part of the season, it being the route by which I proposed to attempt my next discovery, across the mountains from the source of that river [the Peace]; for whatever distance I could reach this fall, would be a proportionate advancement of my voyage." The record is silent on how many went with Mackenzie. He says only that he was "accompanied by two canoes laden with the necessary articles for trade." Each of these canoes carried a crew of five or six. Thus, including Mackenzie, some dozen went forward to Peace River.

Mackenzie traveled first to the Peace River or, as the natives called it, Unjigah or Unchaga River. The Peace may be North America's oldest river, for its rocky bed is said to predate the great eruptions that created the Rocky Mountains. The origins of the river, in the glacier-fed Finlay and Parsnip Rivers, lie west of the Continental Divide. Flowing eastward out of present-day British Columbia, the waters of the Peace then shape a gigantic curve in the area of present-day Peace River Town, Alberta, and then flow north and later east, draining into the Slave River near Lake Athabasca. In a sense, therefore, the Peace is an upland extension of the Mackenzie River. Peace River stood at the leading edge of westward expansion of Canadian trade. Mackenzie entered an area already penetrated, though only recently, by fellow Canadian traders. In 1788 Nor'Wester Charles Boyer had built the first post on the Peace, which others called the Old Establishment, near the mouth of the river that bears his name. The surveyor M. Vaudreuil plotted the river's course as far as Boyer's Post the same summer that Mackenzie made his Arctic tour. Thus, Mackenzie was traversing known ground when he embarked for the Pacific in late 1792. His voyage upriver from Fort Chipewyan was against swift current for about 550 miles to where the Nor'Westers had put up their most distant, westerly places of trade—a string of posts above Fort Vermilion.

In the course of his passage upriver to his intended winter quarters, Mackenzie and his party first moved through level country where waters frequently overflowed their banks. Soon they came upon Peace Point. Here, at some time in the past, the Cree—or, as they were known to the French, the Kristinaux—and the Beaver peoples had settled an ancient, bitter quarrel. On his map Mackenzie drew the war routes of the indigenous rivals of yesteryear. The weather soon grew cold and raw. Mackenzie drove the expedition on, past the Rapid. Soon the canoes were moving in a southwestern direction. On 20 October they reached the New Establishment. This was Fort du Tremble, otherwise known as Old Aspen House or Finlay's Post, situated about forty-six miles upstream of the present Fort Vermilion.

Mackenzie's arrival at the New Establishment had been keenly anticipated. John Finlay, in charge of the place, had

prepared an elaborate welcome for the exploring party. Mackenzie recounted:

> At six o'clock in the morning of the 20th, we landed before
> the house amidst the rejoicing and firing of the people, who
> were animated with the prospect of again indulging themselves
> in the luxury of rum, of which they had been deprived since
> the beginning of May; as it is a practice throughout the North-
> West, neither to see or give any rum to the natives during the
> summer. . . . [T]hey [the natives] all arrived. . . . As they very
> soon expressed their desire of the expected regale, I called
> them together, to the number of forty-two hunters, or men
> capable of bearing arms, to offer some advice, which would be
> equally advantageous to them and to us, and I strengthened
> my admonition with a nine gallon cask of reduced rum and a
> quantity of tobacco. At the same time I observed, that as I
> should not often visit them, I had instanced a greater degree
> of liberality than they had been accustomed to.

Here was the fluid diplomacy of the fur trade at work, with
native demands and trader requirements brought together
through the necessary inducement. Partners in enterprise
were endeavoring to assure each other's loyalty.

Winter came on suddenly. Mackenzie was obliged to press
on from this thriving post and the Eastern Beaver peoples
toward the place intended as "my winter residence." He
had already sent supply canoes ahead of him. The ice now
crowded in on the river. Cold, disagreeable weather made
the passage one of extreme endurance. Mackenzie did not
mention the fatigue he must have felt when he reached his
interim destination; typically, he reported only that his men
were quite exhausted. His survey notes became erratic at
this stage, indicating extreme haste. His route had taken
him up the Peace River, past a temporary post called
McLeod's Fort that Alexander McLeod had erected in 1791
or 1790 near the mouth of the Whitemud. His description
of his zig-zag route, written into his journal to allow him

later to draw the course of the river, is mind-boggling in its elaboration, and the reader is happy to find Mackenzie safely arrived at his destination on the first of November. His location was still on the Peace River, six miles upriver from where the East Branch, or Smoky River, flows into the larger waterway, and above where the Cree warpath crossed overland to Lesser Slave Lake.

Mackenzie's Peace River winter quarters of 1792–93 became known as Fort Fork. Situated so as to attract the northern, upriver native traffic, while similarly serving the Smoky River trade, Fort Fork stood on the east or right bank of the mighty Peace. Here abundant timber gave every advantage to those erecting a stout wilderness bivouac. The benchlike site, relatively open in comparison to most of the lands that encroached on the river channel, stood on a slight elevation overlooking the river. Prevailing winds from the northwest offered reprieve against hungry mosquitoes. Across the stream, here measuring a quarter of a mile wide, lay extensive and beautiful meadows, a splendid parkland abounding with grazing animals, with groves of poplar interspersed on the grasslands. Beyond this agreeable landscape, so pleasing and harmonious to Mackenzie's eye, lay the western mountains, the Rockies, a few days' travel away. Upon reaching the mountains, Mackenzie intended to find his way through some pass or other to the Pacific beyond the upper reaches of the river where he was now camped.

Upon Mackenzie's arrival, the exploring party aimed to be housed for the winter as quickly as possible. Peace River winters are clear, cold, and stimulating. Mackenzie had plenty of provisions, so his tired men could be well fed while they undertook the demanding task of erecting the buildings. Two men had been sent forward the previous spring as an advance party to clear the ground, cut palisades, and square housing timbers.

The traders built Fork Fort on substantial lines. Macken-

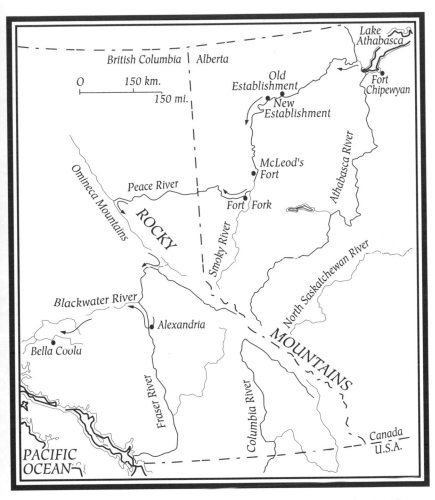

3. Mackenzie's westward route from Fort Chipewyan to the Pacific, showing his 1792–93 winter haven, Fort Fork, on the Peace River.

zie said that it was "a square spot of a hundred and twenty feet" and that the palisades were eighteen feet high and stood in a ditch three feet deep. Mackenzie's house measured twenty-four feet by thirty-eight and had two chimneys, one of which now stands in the grounds of the Peace River Centennial Museum and Archives. There was a warehouse fifteen by ninety feet, divided into three apartments, and a row of five attached houses, each measuring twelve by seventeen feet. Although floods and ice breakups have damaged the site, leaving little to see, visitors can still locate Mackenzie's fort and its remaining trenches and cellars—though the entangling bush and forest seems to wish to recapture the site for nature for all time.

Seventy natives and their chief awaited the traders. Upon seeing them, Mackenzie immediately pulled out some Brazilian tobacco, gave a dram of spirits, and offered the pipe—for he had heard that these natives had been troublesome to his predecessor, McLeod. Mackenzie related how his forest diplomacy proceeded:

> I informed them that I had heard of their misconduct, and was come among them to inquire into the truth of it. I added also that it would be an established rule with me to treat them with kindness, if their behaviour should be such as to deserve it; but, at the same time, that I should be equally severe if they failed in those returns which I had a right to expect from them. I then presented them with a quantity of rum, which I recommended to be used with discretion; and added some tobacco, as a token of peace. They, in return, made me the fairest promises; and, having expressed the pride they felt on beholding me in their country, took their leave.

Here was the fur trader's native policy in miniature, and although some teetotallers like David Thompson refused to dole out spirits to the natives, Mackenzie's measures were generally the order of the day. Liquor and tobacco were a necessary inducement to labor and peace, cooperation and accord, as the records of Nor'Westers Alexander Henry the Younger and Duncan McGillivray testify. The frontier diplomacy that Mackenzie was working out here was that of ancient custom deriving from the earliest years of the *coureurs de bois*.

Settling matters with the natives occupied the first several days at Fort Fork. The traders needed to ensure their winter hunting, not only for the advancement of the trade but also for Mackenzie's benefit and the financing of the expedition. Meanwhile, men of the party had completed the stout stockade and finished the main house. Two days before Christmas Mackenzie shifted from his tent to his habitation, while the men put together another five dwellings within the enclosure. A historian and surveyor of the various North West Company posts on the Peace River, J. N. Wallace, summarizes the military and trading disposition of traders such as McLeod and Mackenzie as follows:

> The site of the post was more than 550 miles from Fort Chipewyan. . . . Courage and tact of no ordinary degree were needed to take charge of so isolated a post. The task of a winterer was not to command a military garrison in a strong fort, but to carry on a trade which was entirely dependent on avoiding conflict with superior numbers who, nonetheless, had to be kept under control. The Indians could, at almost any time, destroy the whole party, and they had to be controlled by moral force. Those from the Highlands of Scotland who had been leaders in their own country, were well fitted for such a task. Self-dependent, inured to Spartan conditions, accustomed to scattered communities, their character was suited to their new surroundings, and the clan system, whatever may have been its faults, certainly produced men who knew how to rule in their own small circle.

But all of the credit did not go to the Scots. Snug in his dwelling, Mackenzie pondered the strength of the Canadians, the packers and the voyageurs, and their willingness to undergo hardships without a murmur. The Canadians had become near transcontinental travelers, he wrote in admiration:

> The men who were now with me, left this place in the beginning of last May, and went to the Rainy Lake in canoes, laden with

packs of fur, which, from the immense length of the voyage, and other concurring circumstances, is a most severe trial of patience and perseverance: there they do not remain a sufficient time for ordinary repose, when they take a load of goods in exchange, and proceed on their return, in a great measure, day and night. They had been arrived [at the site of Fort Fork] near two months, and, all that time, had been continually engaged in very toilsome labour, with nothing more than a common shed to protect them from the frost and snow. Such is the life which these people lead; and is continued with unremitting exertion, till their strength is lost in premature old age.

Mackenzie's comments on the backbone of the northern trade were prescient, for his was not only an exploration of landscape and obstacles, but also of his traveling companions and the peoples he met along the way.

The quietness of winter months provided its own strange and particular blessing. It allowed the explorer the rare opportunity to put on paper many particulars, as he saw them, of the natives of Peace River. Containing valuable insights, these observations are among the best early written descriptions of peoples whose descendants even today are strongly attached to their homeland. Mackenzie, no trained ethnologist, nonetheless took pains to record particulars of the natives with whom he worked and lived.

The bands Mackenzie lived among that winter had suffered at the hands of the more warlike Cree and Beaver, who had pushed them north and west. They seem to have been remnants of groups that had once been stronger, and they lived in insecurity and fear. Mackenzie found them courageous and generous as well as strong and full of gratitude. On one occasion he dressed an appalling thumb wound of a young Indian whose gun had burst. At another moment he commented on the hardships of native women: "It is not uncommon, while the men carry nothing but a gun, that their wives and daughters follow with such weighty burdens, that if they lay them down they cannot replace them, and that is a kindness which the men will not deign to perform; so that during their journeys they are frequently obliged to lean against a tree for a small portion of temporary relief." And again: "It is by no means uncommon in the hasty removal of their camps from one position to another, for a woman to be taken in labour, to deliver herself in her way, without any assistance or notice from her associates in the journey, and to overtake them before they complete the arrangements of their evening station, with her new-born babe on her back." The natives, said Mackenzie, were superstitious. Of one individual, who had lost the power in his legs five years before, Mackenzie recounted: "This affliction he attributed to his cruelty about that time, when having found a wolf with two whelps in an old beaver lodge, he set fire to it and consumed them."

Mackenzie's ethnographic notes are pinned closely to his commercial pursuits, but they are not merely informed by his quest for an empire of profit. He took pains to recount the history of the natives:

> The Indians informed me, that they had been to hunt at a large lake, called by the Knisteneaux, the Slave Lake, which derived its name from that of its original inhabitants, who were called Slaves. They represented it as a large body of water, and that it lies about one hundred and twenty miles due East from this place. It is well known to the Knisteneaux, who are among the inhabitants of the plains on the banks of the Saskatchiwine river; for formerly, when they used to come to make war in this country, they came in their canoes to that lake, and left them there; from thence there is a beaten path all the way to the Fork, or East branch of this river, which was their war-road.

These natives gave useful information, for the river was the way to Lesser Slave Lake, about sixty-five miles southeast of Fort Fork, and hitherto unknown to the Nor'Westers, and the "East branch" was the Smoky River.

Among the natives were two "Rocky Mountain Indians," who resided on the eastern slope of the Rockies. They were probably Sekani, and they came as emissaries of trade, solicitors to bring the Nor'Westers within their sphere of business. They sought to discredit the rivals. They claimed that the other natives with whom Mackenzie then had close relations were entirely ignorant of the geography of the foothills and knew nothing of the lands adjacent to the mountains or of the course and navigation of the Peace River. They stated that the Beaver Indians had encroached upon the Sekani, forcing them to retire to the foot of the Rocky Mountains.

They represented themselves as the only real natives of that country then with me; and added, that the country, and that part of the river that intervenes between this place and the mountains, bear much the same appearance as that around us; that the former abounds with animals, but that the course of the latter is interrupted, near and in the mountains, by successive rapids and considerable falls. These men also informed me, that there is another great river towards the mid-day sun, whose current runs in that direction, and that the distance from it is not great across the mountains.

This was extremely important information: that a great river lay not far beyond the Rockies. Rapids and falls lay farther up the Peace, they warned, but beyond the mountain ramparts coursed a great river.

What wild visions chased through Mackenzie's mind during this winter can only be imagined. Here, near the ramparts of the Rockies, common sense might have indicated the impossibility of a northwest passage. Would the canoe, vehicle of fur traders' triumph over the North American wilderness, here reach the limits of utility? Here, near the continental divide, if a riverway could not be found, the grandest of all portages must exist. For the present, the party's birchbark canoes lay idle. All travel was done on foot, preferably by snowshoe, and even then only on the still and white frozen river that slumbered below the encampment. It was a time of waiting and worrying.

At last, by the beginning of May, the weather grew warm enough to allow Mackenzie to complete final preparations for his western journey and make arrangements for sending furs outward to Fort Chipewyan. The leader ordered all the canoes to be repaired and had four new ones built. He had six canoes sent eastward, loaded with furs and provisions. He retained six men to bolster the western party and engaged some hunters. Mackenzie now wrapped up his accounts for the trading year. He completed his correspondence and sent his dispatches to his partners and to the North West Company. He was as ready as could be. Now his mind raced forward to those circumstances over which he would have no control.

Mackenzie's *Voyages from Montreal* at this juncture fails to tell anything of his concerns. In reading his letter of 8 May 1793 to cousin Roderick, however, we gain a good understanding of what passed through his mind. Here he revealed abundantly his deepest anxieties. "I have been so vexed and disturbed in mind since the beginning of this month that I cannot sit down to any thing steadily. The Indians in general have disappointed me in their hunt. I have had great trouble to procure young men to go along with me—none of them like the voyage." He explained, "I at last got three and a fourth wanted to join but I would not take him, and to be revenged he debauched my guide, and both deserted last night. The two remaining lads know no more of the country than I do myself, and perhaps they are on the eve of playing the same trick, for there is no dependence to be put on the promises of any of these people—and without Indians I have very little hopes of succeeding."

Mackenzie intended to find his way out of the Peace River basin. Therein lay the problem, for the native who had deserted had been on another very large river to the west of the Peace, about two days' march distant. Mackenzie determined to press on regardless, for he was too far along to abandon the attempt. The demands of exploring were not Mackenzie's sole concern. He was constantly perplexed by his relations with other traders, ever concerned about his situation in the firm. On the one hand, he pondered returning to Grand Portage to protect his interests; on the other, he considered staying in the high country and pursuing his ancient plan of finding the route to the western sea. "I never was so undecided in my intentions as this year, regarding my going to the Portage or remaining in land," he confided to Roderick. "I weighed every thing in my mind and over again." Isolation pressed in upon him, and fretfulness became his constant companion. The winter's solitude had brought only added anxiety. So great was Mackenzie's fur-trading acumen that he knew that McTavish could not injure him without doing damage to himself. This did not concern him particularly. What rankled most was his troublesome business affairs with Peter Pangman, evidently up in the air, and he instructed Roderick to have these cleared up. The details are not known, but Pangman, an independent New Englander and a vigorous frontier trader, did not have easy relations with other key partners in the then evolving North West Company.

With this weight on my mind, and wishing to mix in the business at the Portage, I would not have remained, had I any intention of continuing in this country beyond the ensuing winter. Should I be successful I shall retire to greater advantage. Should I not be successful I cannot be worse off than I am at present. I begin to think it is the height of folly in a man to reside in a country of this kind, deprived of every comfort that can render life agreeable, especially when he has a competency to enjoy life in civilized society which will or ought to be the case with me at that time.

Mackenzie's impending departure from his winter head-quarters came as a relief. The journey promised new scenery, unknown dangers, physical demands, and unexpected challenges. The wayfarer needed to be on guard against bears and ambush, famine and accidents. The sedentary life at the post could now be left behind. The wilderness had its own dynamics and its own requirements for human survival. This first European camping expedition into the Canadian Rockies was undertaken without maps showing native trails. The forest-choked creeks threatened to rip birch bark from canoe ribs and throw trinkets and gunpowder into surging waters. As Mackenzie admitted, he was on native sufferance, always dependent on native goodwill. He moved into an unknown native domain, proceeding from the Alberta foothills and mountain ramparts into the lands of the far western and Pacific peoples, the jurisdictions of some of the most powerful and warlike natives of North America. He was entering lands where Kootenai, Shuswap, Blackfoot, and others had crossed and recrossed mountain passes for generations. In slightly more southerly latitudes, David Thompson and Alexander Henry the Younger faced considerable native resistance a decade and a half later.

In such circumstances as Mackenzie and his men were bound to experience, most of the party expressed grave doubts about the expedition and feared for their safety. "My winter interpreter," wrote Mackenzie, "with another person whom I left here to take care of the fort and supply the natives with ammunition during the summer, shed tears on the reflection of those dangers which we might encounter in our expedition, while our own people offered up their prayers that we might return in safety from it."

For the purposes of his western expedition, Mackenzie had ordered the construction of a bark canoe measuring twenty-five feet in length exclusive of the curves of stem and stern. The vessel was strong but so light that it could be carried on a good road by two men for three or four miles without the men resting. In this slender vessel were shipped provisions, presents for the natives, arms, ammunition, and baggage—to a total of a ton and a half—and "an equipage of ten people . . . with two Indians as hunters and interpreters."

Accompanying Mackenzie on the westward journey was his greatest asset, the unheralded Alexander MacKay, or McKay. About eight years younger than Mackenzie, and hence about twenty-two at this time, MacKay was a Loyalist who hailed from the Mohawk Valley and Glengarry County, Upper Canada. Like Mackenzie's father, MacKay's father had been a soldier; he fought for King George at Quebec in 1759. Mackenzie, who already knew of Alexander MacKay, had requested his transfer to Fort Fork because he knew the younger man would provide valuable services to the expedition. MacKay was a natural-born scout, a daring woodsman and tireless canoeist. A contemporary, Gabriel Franchère, called MacKay a brave and enterprising fellow. Courageous and reliable, MacKay became Mackenzie's trusted lieutenant on the great dash to the Pacific. Even so, the explorer could never bring himself to give his righthand man, his "Assistant," his due. However, when Mackenzie made his reluctant decision that he could travel no farther down the raging Fraser, it was MacKay who in an act of homage to the leader carved Mackenzie's name on a tree to mark the southern passage down what was thought to be the great Columbia River. In the end it was MacKay and not Mackenzie who traded on Pacific saltwater.

By a strange turn of events, after MacKay reached the mouth of the Columbia in John Jacob Astor's ship *Tonquin* in 1811, he led an exploring expedition upriver along the course of the stream that Mackenzie had failed to reach in 1793. First to complete the magic double—to go overland to the Pacific and then, as the ranking partner in Astor's

Pacific Fur Company, to round Cape Horn for the northwest coast—MacKay merits a book-length biography. He ended his wild and turbulent western travels at the hands of violent natives. He fell defending the *Tonquin* from a native attack somewhere on the Vancouver Island coast, most probably at Clayoquot Sound. Struck on the head, he was then cast into the sea, where native women in canoes viciously flailed at him with their paddles. MacKay had forewarned the ship's captain, Jonathan Thorn, to make preparations against a hostile native boarding party. He was habituated to frontier conditions; life in the wilderness had taught him to anticipate every contingency. Expeditions such as Mackenzie's were his training ground.

Mackenzie's exploring expedition consisted of ten persons—himself, MacKay, Joseph Landry and Charles Ducette (who had both accompanied Mackenzie to the Arctic), François Beaulieux, Baptist Bisson, François Courtois, Jacques Beauchamp, and two young Indians—all in one canoe. And a dog came along, too, called simply "our dog."

Going upriver on the Peace from Fort Fork, Mackenzie searched for a portage or passage across the western divide. The river belied its name. The waters surged high and strong owing to the melting of the snow. We now know that Mackenzie unfortunately missed the comparatively easy portage known as Giscome and took a more awkward route by way of the Parsnip River, southern tributary of the Peace. Here his distance measurements were grossly underestimated, and it would be left to other traders and explorers, particularly David Thompson, to put down a more accurate record. Within four years of Mackenzie's transit, John Finlay explored Peace River's headwaters, and a year or two later the first Rocky Mountain Fort stood just west of the Continental Divide, presaging a breaching of the mountain ramparts by trade from the east. This was rich fur country. In a few more years the Nor'Westers were anchored on the

Peace from Lake Athabasca to the mountains and held the river in trading fee. Though tributary to Lake Athabasca, the Peace formed a western conduit of empire, and through it, after Mackenzie, went John Finlay, John Stuart, Simon Fraser, and others. Even though Alexander Mackenzie was a transient on the Peace, crossing first westerly and then easterly all in one season, he kept an eye out for trading prospects. Thus, when he independently developed a new business strategy a few years later, Peace River became a battleground between his concern and any rivals. In 1803, for example, Mackenzie's XY Company built a post 100 yards above the Nor'Westers' Fort Fork, as the two concerns struggled for the supremacy of the Peace.

All that lay in the future. For the moment Mackenzie faced numerous impassable rapids. "We . . . continued our toilsome and perilous progress with the line West by North, and as we proceeded the rapidity of the current increased, so that in the distance of two miles we were obliged to unload four times, and carry everything but the canoe." After once again nearly losing the canoe to the rocks, the men were in such a state of alarm that they began to murmur about the necessity of turning back, for "the river above us, as far as we could see, was one white sheet of foaming water." Mackenzie ordered the men to make camp, while he and one of the natives reconnoitered ahead. He sent MacKay and some men in another direction to seek the lay of the land; they found themselves only in the middle of a thick wood. Depression could have descended on them all. Again Mackenzie called on the men for all their strength and dedication, and he did so with the usual inducements of the fur trader. He put it this way: "[A] kettle of wild rice, sweetened with sugar, which had been prepared for their return, with their usual regale of rum, soon renewed that courage which disdained all obstacles that threatened our progress: and they went to rest, with a full determination to surmount them on the morrow."

By 21 May the party had come to the perpendicular ramparts of the Rockies. When necessary, Mackenzie took to the riverbanks and held the tow rope that kept the canoe from disaster. But on at least one occasion that rope broke, and the canoe with its precious cargo was swept down the rapids. Miraculously, the vessel came to rest on a safe bank, where the men, who had gone below to await the canoe, pulled it up onto narrow rocks. The men, growing desperate, talked of mutiny. The paddlers would go no further. Mackenzie again brought out the rum. While the voyageurs were thinking the matter over, Mackenzie clambered up the rocks and found a portage in two parts that would get around a nine-mile rapids. The men were persuaded to carry on.

Bright, cold weather had given way to violent rain. Mackenzie and the men kept to their rain-drenched camp on 29 May and downed nearly a keg of rum. In his journal entry for that date we read that Mackenzie amused himself that day by writing a brief report of all their hardships, which he wrapped in bark and pushed into the bunghole. He then let go the keg on the stream. The next day their dog raised an alarm and ran ceaselessly back and forth at the rear of the party. They discovered that a wolf was stalking along a ridge a few yards behind them in search of a meal. They were perhaps near Portage Mountain.

Now the mountains presented an even more formidable prospect than they had anticipated. Every time the voyageurs came around a promising bend in the river or spotted a beckoning defile between mountains, they came face to face with yet another impediment to progress. They had come, in fact, to a ridge or chain of mountains that ran north and south as far as the eye could see.

It was now the last day of May, and they were at the confluence of the Finlay and the Parsnip, the great western forks of the Peace known as Finlay Forks. Which river to take? Mackenzie put the dilemma this way:

> If I had been governed by my own judgment, I should have taken the former [the Finlay River], as it appeared to me to be the most likely to bring us nearest to the part where I wished to fall on the Pacific Ocean, but the old man whom I have already mentioned as having been frequently on war expeditions in this country, had warned me not, on any account, to follow it, as it was soon lost in various branches among the mountains, and that there was no great river that ran in any direction near it; but by following the latter, he said, we should arrive at a carrying-place to another large river [the Fraser River], that did not exceed a day's march, where the inhabitants build houses, and live upon islands.

Mackenzie determined to take the old man's advice, for he had no doubt that if he could reach the Fraser, he could reach the Pacific Ocean. He rejected the protests of his men, who argued for the Finlay as being smoother. Native advice is what he leaned on at this juncture.

Now they steered for the Parsnip River—or, as it may be better styled, the South Branch. The stream soon became a wild current, and progress was very tiresome and even mortifying. The condition of his men now concerned the leader, and he commented on "the inexpressible toil these people had endured, as well as the dangers they had encountered." Again he spoke to them, assuaging their fears, calling on their inner strength. They continued, day by day, as current and energy would allow. One of the party, sent ahead, stated positively that he had heard the discharge of firearms above their encampment. They got out the muskets and pistols in readiness. Worries circulated that a party of warlike Cree were in the neighborhood and that they would fall upon the exploring expedition. The men spent an uneasy night, taking turns on guard, muskets in hand, but found the next day that some trees had fallen into the river, which had created the noise that had alarmed them so. Again they continued their passage upriver.

Here Mackenzie met the Sekani, the "People of the Rocks." They belonged to the Beaver-Sarcee-Sekani branch of the Athabaskans, who lived in the mountainous areas of present-day British Columbia drained by the Finlay and Parsnip branches of the Peace River. The band met by Mackenzie was probably the same as those called Big Men by a Nor'West trader in 1806. They numbered ten families, about fifty people, when Mackenzie met them. They informed him that they knew of no great river to the westward, but that there existed a river across an eleven-day carrying-place, and that same river was the one that they were now standing beside. In fact, the Sekani, who traveled in family groups on their regular hunting rounds, had just arrived from its western reaches. They recounted how they traded with people to the west, who in turn traveled "during a moon" to get to the country of other tribes, who lived in houses. They also reported that these same neighbors journeyed even to the seacoast and to what they called "the Stinking Lake." In that distant place people like Mackenzie—that is to say, Europeans—traded, arriving in vessels as big as islands. The Sekani had other information to offer Mackenzie: They had heard from other natives farther west of a stream following toward the noonday sun, a waterway that eventually flowed to the "stinking waters." The people to the westward were very numerous, reported the Sekani.

Mackenzie now digested this new intelligence. He had no reason to doubt the Sekani advice, for these people seemed well informed. Indeed, anthropological evidence reveals that they had vast trading networks and alliances. Mackenzie was troubled, however, by the report of this river, which seemed to cross the mountains. The whole weight of this native advice, as he expressed it, "threatened to disconcert the project on which my heart was set, and in which my whole mind was occupied." He was lost in a mountain river trench and had mutiny rising among his men. He promised presents and renewed trade if he could get one of the Sekani to act as guide. However, they lived in fear of the Beaver people, who were more warlike and more numerous. Mackenzie's efforts at persuasion meant nothing to them. "They still persisted in their ignorance of any such river as I had mentioned, that discharged itself into the sea."

It may be that all voyages of great historical significance experience at least one great crisis—for instance, a stormy doubling of Cape Horn. Reading Mackenzie's *Voyages from Montreal* page by page, the armchair traveler reads of so many crises that he or she may become dulled to the magnitude of the expedition's difficulties. Tucked in the middle of Mackenzie's narrative of his Rocky Mountain passage (crossing from today's Alberta into British Columbia and at last out of the headwaters of Peace River) are paragraphs easily passed by in the reader's vicarious race to Pacific shores. They speak volumes of Mackenzie's troubles through "dreadful country" and of his men's fears and terrible circumstances. Related in the anodyne language of the eighteenth century, they dull our senses nowadays. But they should not go unnoticed.

After hearing what the Sekani had to say, Mackenzie wrote with dismay:

> In this state of perplexity and disappointment, various projects presented themselves to my mind, which were no sooner formed than they were discovered to be impracticable, and were consequently abandoned. At one time I thought of leaving the canoe, and every thing it contained, to go over land, and pursue that chain of connexion by which these people obtain their ironwork; but a very brief course of reflection convinced

me that it would be impossible for us to carry provisions for our support through any considerable part of such a journey, as well as presents, to secure us a kind reception among the natives, and ammunition for the service of the hunters, and to defend ourselves against any act of hostility.

His mind turned to another alternative—going overland by the way the Sekani told of. This possibility he set aside as too time consuming, even if no misfortune overtook the party. Yet going back was unthinkable; a return was "an idea too painful to indulge." All his dreams would have been shattered, his credibility among fellow traders perhaps destroyed, his career possibly in ruin.

In the circumstances, Mackenzie decided that the only suitable course was to wait it out with the Sekani and hope they would divulge their geographical secrets. Next morning he questioned them again, and one of them mentioned something about a great river lying up the river that lay before them. Mackenzie was told of a large river that ran toward the midday sun. A portage across three small lakes would take them to a small stream, and this in turn would discharge into the great river (which did not, they said, run to the sea). Such information now buoyed up Mackenzie's spirits and renewed his hopes. He discounted the Sekani advice that the river could not or did not lead to the sea and concluded that the informant was ignorant of the country. He obtained a guide to conduct him to the first native inhabitants, at the small lakes, and issued orders for the party to prepare for departure. Before long they were in a land of ponds and slow-moving, wandering streams choked with driftwood. They searched in vain for new guides. Then they came to Arctic Lake, fed by snow, and passed through rivulets and a morass that eventually became a stream.

That day, 12 June, a portage over a low ridge to another mountain lake brought them to waters draining west. They were in the Pacific drainage basin at last, west of the Conti-

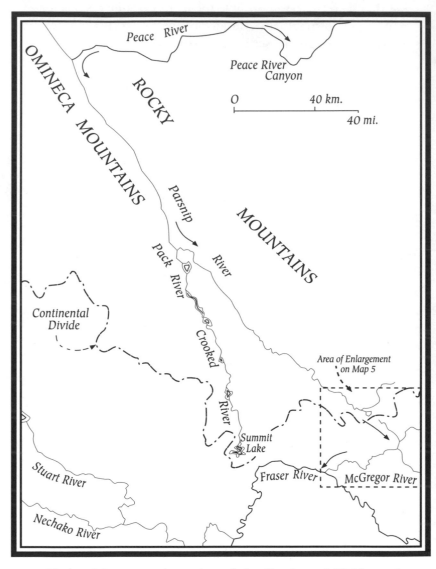

4. Mackenzie's westward crossing of the Continental Divide to the Fraser River, 1793.

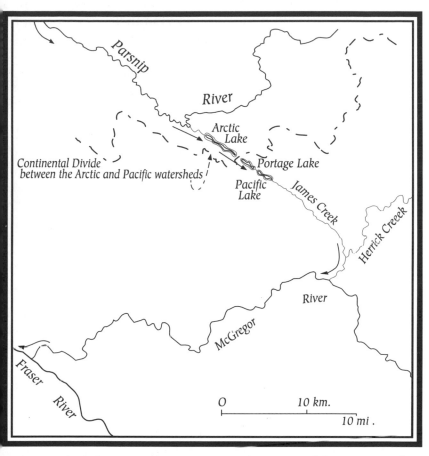

5. Detail of Map 4. Mackenzie's westward crossing of the Continental Divide, 1793.

nental Divide. The reconnoitering party reported in fearful detail some hazards on the stream, and that evening they prepared for the challenges ahead. The next day some of the men began to cut a road, while others loaded the canoe for the passage down the hazards. "In order to lighten [the canoe]," said Mackenzie, "it was my intention to walk with some of the people; but those in the boat with great earnestness requested me to embark, declaring, at the same time, that, if they perished, I should perish with them. I did not then imagine in how short a period their apprehension would be justified." They pushed off, and the canoe struck and was then swung sideways down the river toward a bar that threatened to destroy it and scatter the cargo. Mackenzie leaped over the gunwales, and the men followed. They desperately tried to straighten the craft but failed, and as the water deepened they realized that they would have to climb back in or lose the canoe altogether. They careened against one rock, ripping the stern, and shot across to the other bank, this time causing damage to the bow. MacKay, the foreman, grabbed an overhanging tree limb in a vain attempt to anchor the craft. He was thrown ashore. They shot down the cascade, tearing large holes in the canoe bottom, and it was this, strange to say, which actually saved them all, for the wreck became flat on the water and they were all able to jump out, cling to the gunwales, and ride the whitewater for several hundred yards into shallow water. All of this passed in a matter of minutes. The voyageurs ashore came to the rescue, but the natives, "when they saw our deplorable situation, instead of making the least effort to help us, sat down and gave vent to their tears." Mackenzie was numbed by the cold of the water, and he was so fatigued that it was some time before he could stand.

They had lost all their stock of balls in the accident but had saved the powder and some shot. The canoe was a wreck. In rapid succession Mackenzie's men dried the ammunition, sent parties to cut portages or find a way, and sought new information to ease their passage. Eventually they fixed upon making a thirty-foot birch-bark canoe. This would be larger than its predecessor and would enable them to carry all the rolled-up birch bark and other repair supplies they were likely to need, for they were now moving into a forest where birch trees were somewhat scarce. The native guide was troubled and dissatisfied; Mackenzie could get nothing of value from him and was instead treated to "strange, fanciful, but terrifying descriptions of the natives" in the country that lay ahead. Mackenzie knew the guide's loyalty was lapsing, and he feared losing him altogether. At night he and MacKay took turns keeping an eye on the guide, but on 17 June the man made his escape from under MacKay's nose. MacKay received Mackenzie's rebuke, and following urgent orders he went with a native, accompanied by the dog, in search of the guide, who could not be found. In any event, the lack of a guide did not slow Mackenzie's progress, and traveling alternately by land and by water they came after some toil across a neck of land to the bank of the great river. "At length we enjoyed, after all our toil and anxiety, the inexpressible satisfaction of finding ourselves on the bank of a navigable river, on the West side of the first great range of mountains."

Relief descended over Mackenzie, a calm upon turbulent waters of the mind. At least the river had been found. For the time being that was enough. What sort of progress had the exploring expedition made to date? Thirty days had passed between their setting out from Fort Fork and their arrival on the banks of the river of the West. They had traveled about four hundred miles in that time, an average progression of thirteen miles a day, half the average speed of Mackenzie's Arctic adventure. After the first ten days they had reached the Rockies and crossed the height of land that was the Continental Divide. They were now on a tributary of the Fraser River.

Once upon the river, the party surged forth on the current, which increased as they advanced. Soon they were lost in a larger branch, the McGregor, which in turn joined a large river, the Fraser. Thus Herrick Creek, at it is now called, had become the Upper McGregor River, the North Fork of the Fraser River. Mackenzie was the first nonnative to see the Fraser River, though at the time he believed himself

to be on the Columbia River, the mouth of which had been
discovered in 1792 by Robert Gray, sailing in the Boston
sea otter trading vessel *Columbia*. From natives Mackenzie
learned their name for the Fraser: Tacoutche-Desse, a com-
bined Carrier and Dene term meaning, literally, "Mouth-
River."

A considerable distance along the Fraser River, Mackenzie
and his men stopped to talk to natives. Migratory fishers
and hunters, some of them had wild and ferocious appear-
ances, said Mackenzie in his commentary for 22 June. He
worried that his guides would be killed. In fact, the strangers
came, one by one, to visit with Mackenzie. They were altogether welcoming. "I shook hands with them all, and desired
my interpreters to explain that salutation as a token of friendship." The natives, sixteen men and some women, extended
a genial invitation to pass the night at their lodges nearby.
They promised the next morning to send two men to introduce Mackenzie's party to the next nation, who were numerous and ill-disposed toward strangers. Mackenzie was startled to hear the Cree language spoken by one of the women,
and on inquiry he learned that she had been taken prisoner
by the Cree, who had carried her across the mountains but
had been captured by a war party of these people, the Sekani.
She had no cause to complain of her present husband, who
detained her, Mackenzie noted, but she said that she wanted
to return to her kin. Mackenzie gave her several useful
articles and told her to come to him at the lodges, which
she agreed to do. He sought to gain information from her
about the country beyond.

At the lodges they found a large group of people, about
thirty-five in all. The prisoner could not be found among
them, and Mackenzie was disappointed that she did not
make her appearance. He concluded that she had been secreted away, so that the Europeans could not take her with
them. Mackenzie gave out as many presents as he could and

then settled into the usual attempt to extract information about his whereabouts and the road to the Pacific. He was then at the extremity of his descent on the Fraser River, in the vicinity of Alexandria, where in 1821 the Nor'Westers built a post and named it in his honor.

That night in camp proved to be a gold mine of information for the knowledge-hungry leader. In addition to the Sekani, there were four men from the neighboring Shuswap people and a woman, a Rocky Mountain Indian, probably a Sekani, who had been with this band for some time. This person became the intermediary in a multilingual exchange that passed back and forth from Mackenzie through the interpreters and to the hosts and their Shuswap visitors. Mackenzie was able to get as much information as they could supply. He chose an elderly man from among the four strangers as the target for his inquiries. Mackenzie explained to the Shuswap the intention of his expedition and the great advantages they would receive from its successful conclusion, by which he meant trade. They were pleased to know his intentions and gave assurance that they would not deceive him. An elderly chief urged him to return again to his land and promised his two daughters to him. Mackenzie returned to the other old man and asked him to draw a map on a large piece of bark. The old man set to work, sought the counsel of his allies when required, and eventually described the Fraser River as running to the east of south and receiving many rivers. He said that it was very hazardous, being filled with impassable rapids. Beyond the necessary portages and the lands of three other tribes, who spoke different languages, lay open country, abounding in deer, which would take Mackenzie to a lake that contained water that the natives did not drink. The old man talked of the trade from that quarter and soon produced a ten-inch knife with a handle of horn "obtained from white men." "One very old man observed, that as long as he could remember, he was told of white people to the Southward; and that he had heard, though he did not vouch for the truth of the report, that one of them had made an attempt to come up the river, and was destroyed." Perhaps a runaway from a vessel trading in sea otter had sought to ascend the river and had been killed. Or perhaps it is a reference to one of the Spaniards reported to have visited the south Okanagan area. No other written record confirms this fascinating scrap of oral testimony taken by Mackenzie.

Mackenzie now had to consider his situation. His informants declared it was a short distance across the country west to the Pacific. How short was this distance, Mackenzie wondered. In 1790 the mariner John Meares had speculated in his publication *Voyages Made in the Years 1788 and 1789 from China to the North-West Coast of America* that there was a northwest passage in this exact area; Mackenzie knew of this claim, and he may even have carried a copy of Meares's book (or his wildly speculative chart) in his pack. If Meares's assertion was correct, reasoned Mackenzie, then the ocean could not be as far as the "inland sea" that Meares had mentioned as lying to the east of Nootka Sound. At this stage neither Meares nor Mackenzie had the geographical details right.

"After going down it [the Fraser River] about 420 miles [from where he believed the river to commence]," he recounts in his Journal, "I learned from the Natives that as far as they had any knowledge of it, it went a Southern course. From their description and my own observations I concluded it to be a part or the whole of the River of the West." He thought that it was the Columbia River.

How far should he go on this stream? Mackenzie pondered his situation and had to make a difficult choice between going south by water or west by land. Although he was on what he thought to be the fabled great western stream, he concluded that the distance to its mouth would be too great to go there and back in one season. He would have to take time to build a stouter vessel for such a hazardous river run. Mackenzie, like Lewis and Clark a decade later, worried about the supply of game in the wooded mountain West, which stood in sharp contrast to the bounty of prairie game. Mackenzie's party had lost all their bullets upon which depended the killing of deer. Thoughts of hunger and starvation passed through the leader's mind as he continued to ponder the options.

Mackenzie considered the overland alternative. Natives gave him to understand, as he stated wryly, that he was "not far overland to the Sea." Following their instructions he paddled some eighty miles upriver. He cached his canoe in latitude 53°N, longitude 122°43′W. Mackenzie penned in his Journal: "I have not the least doubt of this great River being navigable with Canoes and boats to its Mouth. I have mentioned above the cause of my not putting this to the proof. It abounds in Salmon and other fish, is well inhabited. They clothe themselves in fur and skins and live by fishing and hunting."

And what if he had taken the southern water? Then as now the Fraser River offered no one an easy journey. Simon Fraser on his grand reconnaissance of 1806 found treacherous whitewater and canyons impossible to portage. Wisely taking native advice, he bypassed obstacles such as Hell's Gate and finally reached navigable freshwater that led to the saltwater estuary just north of latitude 49°N (on the Fraser at South Vancouver). Of the river that Mackenzie had chosen to sidestep thirteen years earlier, Fraser wrote:

I have been for a long period in the Rocky Mountains, but have never seen anything like this country. It is so wild that I cannot find words to describe our situation at times. We had to pass where no human beings should venture; yet in those places there is a regular footpath impressed, or rather indented upon the very rocks by frequent travelling. Besides this, steps which are formed like a ladder . . . furnish a safe and convenient passage to the natives; but we, who had not had the advantage of their education and experience, were often in imminent danger when obliged to follow their example.

Fraser persisted, for he had been instructed to descend the river, and he intended to follow his instructions. "Going to the sea by an indirect way," he wrote, "was not the object of this undertaking; I therefore would not deviate and continued our route according to our original intention."

On Sunday 23 June Mackenzie decided to go overland, and he did so, on the banks of this his second river of disappointment, only after reexamining his native informants of the previous day. At that moment he was much surprised by this blunt question from one of the natives: "What can be the reason you are anxious in your inquiries of us respecting a knowledge of this country. Do not you white men know everything in the world?" The native was having a little fun at the explorer's expense. After all, the native knew precisely where he was, while the progress-oriented European was lost and driven to systematize and to "discover." To the explorer this sardonic query was so very unexpected that he hesitated and took a moment to gather his thoughts for an answer. In his reply Mackenzie summed up the differences in perception regarding the physical world between natives and Europeans, telling the man "that we certainly were acquainted with the principal circumstances of every part of the world; that I knew where the sea is, and where I myself then was, but that I did not exactly understand what obstacles might interrupt me in getting to it; with which, he and his relations must be well acquainted, as they had so frequently surmounted them. Thus I fortunately preserved the impression in their minds, of the superiority of white people over themselves." Mackenzie flattered himself in thinking his race enjoyed superiority in that native land, and much of what he said can be classified as bluster. The explorer hoped for additional information, but learned little. The natives did offer an insight of special value concerning the West Road River, as Mackenzie called it. This stream, now the Blackwater River in its volcanic bed, lay nearby and offered a route west. By way of it the natives could reach the northwest coast natives, the people with the wooden canoes.

> They continued to inform me, that if I went that way we must leave our own canoe behind us; but that they thought it probable that those people would furnish us with another. From thence they stated the distance to be only one day's voyage with the current to the lake whose water is nauseous, and where they had heard that great canoes came two winters ago, and that the people belonging to them, brought great quantities of goods and built houses.

Maritime fur-trading vessels, at least a dozen, were sailing the northwest coast in these years. Natives of the interior reconfirmed for Mackenzie the impact of trade goods.

Later that same day Mackenzie summoned his nine exhausted, hungry people. It was time for a chat. "After passing a warm eulogium on their fortitude, patience and perseverance," as he said, he got to the heart of the matter:

> I stated the difficulties that threatened our continuing to navigate the river, the length of time it would require, and the scanty provisions we had for such a voyage: I then proceeded for the foregoing reasons to propose a shorter route, by trying the over-land road to the sea. . . . I declared my resolution not to attempt it unless they would engage, if we could not after all proceed over land, to return with me, and continue our voyage to the discharge of the waters, whatever the distance might be. At all events, I declared, in the most solemn manner,

that I would not abandon my design of reaching the sea, if I
made the attempt alone, and that I did not despair of returning
in safety to my friends.

The men agreed to follow him.

The overland journey would be a simpler affair than the
river run, it is true. However, every minute was critical, for
it was already midsummer and two months had passed since
their departure from Fort Fork. They now had no river as
a guide, but they had instead the promise of a route frequented by natives in going to the Western Ocean, as Mackenzie later told Governor Dorchester. These natives carried
their furs to the northwest coast tribes, and from them in
turn they obtained iron and trinkets. Mackenzie here alluded
to what was known to natives as "the grease trail," where
oil rendered from the *oolichan* (candlefish) was brought into
the mountain interior in exchange for trade goods of more
eastern natives. In fact, not one but several native trails
crossed this terrain, posing for the explorer the dilemma of
which of the various routes to take. Mackenzie took a portion, or portions, of the trail of the Southern Carriers, used
by them for thousands of years. He found this path, now
called the Nuxalk-Carrier grease trail, "very good and well
traced." This is the route now available for retracing by
trackers following the advice of the Alexander Mackenzie
Voyageur Route Association's guidebook *In the Steps of
Alexander Mackenzie*. The distance was farther than advertised, and his guides threatened to quit. Because of the huge
packs they were carrying on their backs, Mackenzie decided
to lighten the load wherever he could. He cached pemmican
for the return journey and then had to reduce daily rations
by one-third. But carry on they did, beside the West Road
River, beyond the Kluskus Lakes, Ulgako Creek, and Eliguk
Lake, and then over a low mountain to Gatcho Lake. There
he found a marvelous large coastal-type house clad in planks,
expertly fashioned and decorated.

Once out of swamp and shallow stream, they came to a place where they could put together a raft and crossed a river, the Dean. Had they followed that river they would have come to the Pacific at Kimsquit, on Dean Channel. Their guides took them by a different route. Exhausted, Mackenzie and his men made camp early, at nine that evening. "The weather being clear throughout the day, we had no reason to complain of the cold. Our guides encouraged us with the hope that, in two days of similar exertion, we should arrive among the people of the other nation." The next day, 15 July, they were in motion by five o'clock and passed down and across the river. Soon they came upon five families of the Ntshaautin, a Carrier group, whom Mackenzie says called themselves Neguia Dinais. "They received us with great kindness, and examined us with the most minute attention. They must, however, have been told that we were white, as our faces no longer indicated that distinguishing complexion." They, too, were in transit, traveling to coastal rivers. Mackenzie took a shine to these folk, and he gave a sympathetic portrait of a Carrier multifamily cluster who were trading intermediaries between Pacific and interior peoples. Mackenzie admired everything about these people except their slow pace. The women wore their hair in great, neat plaits and knots decorated with beads. The men were clothed in leather, and Mackenzie noted how they had fairer, clearer complexions than any other natives yet seen by the expedition. Their eyes were gray, with a tinge of red, not the customary dark eyes of other natives. Every man, woman, and child carried a burden proportionate to their size. They traveled as a great family, and Mackenzie and his men, accustomed to a torrid pace, enjoyed the comparative slowness of these agreeable and happy companions. They took time for games, and Mackenzie looked on in wonder, taking careful note of a game of skill and chance.

We all sat down on a very pleasant spot and were no sooner seated, than our guide and one of the party prepared to engage in play. They had each a bundle of about fifty small sticks, neatly polished, of the size of a quill, and five inches long: a certain number of these sticks had red lines round them; and as many of these as one of the players might find convenient were curiously rolled up in dry grass, and according to the judgment of his antagonist respecting their number and marks, he lost or won. Our friend was apparently the loser, as he parted with his bow and arrows, and several articles which I had given him.

However, his fellow travelers had no compulsion about a speedy westward passage. Mackenzie worried about his provisions, now in short supply. Although the Ntshaautin assured the explorer's party that they would look after them and that in any case they would soon be at their intended destination, Mackenzie had made up his mind. Soon, too, an advance party brought to camp new guides, and Mackenzie said farewell to these agreeable people.

His entry for 17 July speaks volumes of a new world entered, of a traveler in a land quite unknown to him— different in inhabitants and habitations. Mackenzie was a foreigner from the East. He was soon in splendidly beautiful alpine country, known locally now as the Mackenzie Valley, watered by a small river, the Kohasganko. They trudged along a compacted snow trail and across a 6,000-foot drift-filled pass. They climbed a nearby mountain and found themselves surrounded by snow. The weather, said Mackenzie, was as distressing as any he had ever experienced. Hail, snow, and rain drove upon them in a tempest, and the party shivered with cold and took refuge from the wild and windy storm by hiding in the lee of a huge rock. The hunters, who had expended much ammunition in shooting at a large herd of deer, came back with only a small mountain caribou, blaming their poor aim on weather conditions. It was so cold that the men were glad to take to their trail again and to renew their march. Mackenzie would have been happy to leave behind half the caribou meat, but his men, fearing hunger, insisted that all of it be carried—even though, as Mackenzie explained, their strength was exhausted.

"Before us appeared a stupendous mountain, whose snow-clad summit was lost in the clouds." Mackenzie was now on an alpine plateau looking south to jagged peaks on the far side of the Bella Coola Valley, one of which was Stupendous Mountain. But as he and his men went forward, the mountains, annoyingly, seemed to withdraw from them. As they came to a more open space and got a better view of the horizon, the mountains appeared even higher in their "awful elevation." They continued their descent through the valley until they came to the brink of a precipice. Their guides, said Mackenzie, "discovered the river to us"—that is, showed the way—and there they came upon a riverside village.

Mackenzie and his men stood on the rim of Bella Coola Gorge, some 3,000 feet deep. The view was majestic—a series of precipices covered with large trees and, so they were told, abounding in wildlife, including mountain goats. They descended the gorge in two hours, and at the bottom they came upon two rivers that joined at that spot, the Burnt Bridge Creek and the Bella Coola River. The rivers were swift flowing. The timber was large. Mackenzie inquired from his guides as to why even the highest of the hemlock, which must have been some 300 feet tall, was stripped of bark to the very top. He concluded that the natives used the bark for tanning. He found there the largest alders and cedar he had seen. The berries growing roundabout were ripe. As many another visitor to the Pacific coast could understand, Mackenzie was in a new habitat. "We were now sensible of an entire change in the climate" is the way he put it.

"The sun was about to set when our conductors left us to follow them as well as we could," said Mackenzie. The guides had taken to their heels and left the slower, exhausted traders to follow as best they could. Thickets crowded in upon them. At least the guides marked the trail by breaking tree branches as they passed along the way.

They here breathed moister air, blessed by the Japanese current. They were about to come into a rich and complex world of native peoples the likes of which they had not seen before, a land of cedar inhabited by skilled woodworkers. In this land of contrasts, with its overhanging glaciers, thick forests, and turbulent glacial waters, they were entering the world of the people whom the Kwakiutl called the Bella Coola. These were actually the people of Nuxalk, an enclave of Salish speakers. The Nuxalk lived in independent villages and devoted even more attention to their ceremonial rites than they did to waging war. They were powerful, rich traders and relatively secure far upriver in this splendid fjord-like domain.

In due time Mackenzie came to open ground at the edge of the forest. Before him stood a house, several fires, and villagers cooking fish. What sort of reception would he have, he wondered? They received him without the least appearance of surprise, for the guides going on before had done their work. "[They] made signs for me to go up to a large house, erected on upright posts. I entered the house and was received by several people sitting upon a very wide board. I seated myself beside a man of dignified countenance. In a short time my people arrived and placed themselves near me. The man by whom I sat immediately rose and fetched a quantity of roasted salmon." A bowl of creamlike, pounded salmon roe was brought for them, and "our protector" indicated that the visitors could sleep within the house. For reasons of prudence Mackenzie chose to sleep outside and to make a fire to sleep beside. The protector then placed boards on the ground for his visitors and ordered a fire prepared. "I never enjoyed a more sound and refreshing rest," sighed the explorer, "though I had a board for my bed and a billet for my pillow."

Here at this "Friendly Village," two hundred yards above the present mouth of Burnt Bridge Creek and now hidden in a tangle of rose and gooseberry bushes, Mackenzie was a welcome guest. In the morning when he awoke the fire was already burning, having been lit by the natives. Soon plenty of berries and salmon were produced. Looking around, Mackenzie marveled at the weir placed across the river. Later, Mackenzie requested a canoe. His request was denied when the headman learned that the explorer intended to take meat—probably the remnant of the mountain caribou they had shot in alpine country—in the canoe. This, the host explained, would scare away the fish that were their sole food.

Two canoes arrived, and guides were arranged for a thirty-mile passage by river to the sea. They paddled along at immense speed. They even shot over a weir without taking on a drop of water. "I had imagined that the Canadians who accompanied me were the most expert canoe-men in the world," mused the traveler, now apparently at his ease, "but they are very inferior to these people, as they themselves acknowledged, in conducting those vessels."

Eight or nine miles downstream, at Noosgulch or Nooskulst, Mackenzie came to a "Great Village," also of the Nuxalk people, consisting of four elevated houses and two on the ground, home to at least two hundred people. Mackenzie made his entrance on foot, and his arrival caused great alarm. The inhabitants were well armed, and gave the appearance of hostility. There was much noise and shouting. The explorer gathered his wits and tried to present himself as a visitor without fear. As he made his final approach to the great chief, Mackenzie was surprised and delighted when his host gave him a warm bear hug. Others hugged him in turn. This warm embrace was a formal greeting, and soon a boisterous crowd pressed in close around him. Now the gift exchange began, and a chiefly feast followed. The son of the chief gave Mackenzie his precious sea otter robe and covered him with it. "This was as flattering a reception as I could possible receive, especially as I considered him to be the eldest son of the chief. Indeed it appeared to me that we had been detained here for the purpose of giving him time to bring the robe with which he had presented me." There followed a pleasant tour of the village and much feasting on foods entirely new to the explorer and his men. To return kindnesses, Mackenzie took from his packs various articles, a blanket, and a pair of scissors with which, as Mackenzie explained, the young chief could clip his great beard, which he did. The explorer also distributed gifts to others who had been attentive to them. Communication between the visitors and the hosts was awkward, however, and was carried on only in signs. After undertaking some medical procedures with natives who requested help, Mackenzie hurried to make his departure, sickened as he was by the natives' own treatment of open sores, involving fire, blunt instruments, and cruel pain. On returning to the village the chief showed him

a garment of blue cloth, decorated with brass buttons; and another of flowered cotton, which I suppose were Spanish. . . . Copper and brass are in great estimation among them, and of the former they have a great plenty: they point their arrows and spears with it, and work it up into personal ornaments; such as collars, ear-rings, and bracelets which they wear on their wrists, arms, and legs. . . . The brass is in thin squares; their copper is in larger pieces, and some of it appeared to be old stills cut up. They also abound in iron [made into] poignards and daggers.

Mackenzie's attention turned to the chief's massive canoe. A splendid craft made of cedar and measuring forty-five feet in length, four feet in width, and three and a half feet in depth, it was capable of carrying forty people. Sea otter teeth adorned its gunwales fore and aft, and Mackenzie, who never missed a trick in his search for correct detail, stated adamantly that Captain Cook was quite wrong in noting that the northwest coast natives decorated their canoes with human teeth. The chief said that about ten years before he had voyaged toward the midday sun, where he had seen two large vessels full of men like Mackenzie—that is, Europeans—by whom he had been kindly received. These were the first Europeans the people of Nooskulst had seen. Mackenzie concluded that these were Captain Cook's vessels, the *Resolution* and the *Discovery,* and that perhaps the chief had gone to Nootka Sound in April 1778. Cook's track kept him well off the coast during other times, en route to Cook Inlet, Alaska.

One of Mackenzie's axes was missing, and Mackenzie demanded its restoration. He worried that its loss might soon result in the loss of all his possessions "and of our lives also." The axe, which had been hidden under the chief's canoe, was eventually returned. Mackenzie's men were dissatisfied with him for the moment because of this defiant demand, "but I thought myself right then, and, I think now, that the circumstances in which we were involved, justified the measure which I adopted."

Once they were in the canoe, their river voyage seemed like flying downstream on a raging current and rapid. Shooting past settlements, they stopped at two large houses to pay respects to a chief of considerable importance, and here their wealthy hosts paraded old copper stills. The Europeans saw, for the first time, a woman "with two pieces of copper in her upper lip, as described by Captain Cook." They watched the making of bark cloth and saw women beating cedar bark rind until it looked like flax. Others spun it with distaff and spindles. Another wove it into a robe, working in stripes of sea otter pelt. Back in a canoe, and having feasted on berries, they surged down the narrowing river until they came to a village of six very large and high houses, erected on palisades. This is the place that, as we will later see, Mackenzie was to dub Rascal's Village. Mackenzie determined to camp here, where the course of the river was westerly. He was now on Pacific tidewater. Any excitement that the explorer felt was not transferred to the pages of his narrative. Perhaps exhaustion had taken its toll. Unlike Balboa staring in awed silence at the grand Pacific, this Canadian Scot in workaday fashion simply bedded down for the night.

On 20 July he was up early, coaxing the natives to get a canoe. The natives thought Mackenzie ought to have been satisfied "with having come in sight of the sea." Mackenzie insisted that he had to find its broader waters, and by eight that morning they were out of the broad Bella Coola River delta and into one of the sea fjords, North Bentinck Arm, at the head of Burke Channel. It was low tide, seaweed covered the shoreline, surrounding hills were enveloped in fog, and a strong westerly wind bit into their faces. Sea otters, or more likely seals, offered targets for the musketeers. A white-headed eagle soared overhead. The wind whipped up, and the tidal sea became so boisterous that they steered their leaking canoe for a small cove, Green Bay, on the north side of the channel.

Mackenzie's young native guide now sought to desert. Although he was recaptured by MacKay, Mackenzie saw no point in detaining him. Instead, he gave the guide a few presents, including a pair of shoes and a silk handkerchief, and told him to go inform his friends that the expedition would return in three nights' time. The young man then walked away in the company of the young chief. That night the exploring party feasted on boiled porcupine and wondered what the next day would bring.

Mackenzie now turned to the problem of getting observations, hoping to obtain navigational sightings of the moon and stars, particularly Jupiter with its moons. Heavy overcast skies seemed perpetual and checked this aspect of his progress. Time, too, seemed against him. Provisions were running out. "Our stock was, at this time, reduced to twenty pounds of pemmican, fifteen pounds of rice, and six pounds of flour, among ten half-starved men, in a leaky vessel, on a barbarous coast." How long could he afford to wait for that sighting of the stars that would give transcontinental travelers the first "fix" on that coast in northern latitudes? Nothing was more important to Mackenzie, for he needed this to prove his location to the wider world. Without it, in that age of scientific reason, he might as well have been on another apocryphal voyage of record.

For breakfast on 21 July MacKay produced some seafood—mussels, in fact—which he and Mackenzie feasted on; the Canadians, however, "did not partake in this regale," being unaccustomed to shellfish. Again on the water, they left what they called Porcupine Bay and shaped a course west-southwest for seven miles, and came to an open channel, two and a half miles wide, that presented a broad vista. Mackenzie now realized that he would not see the open Pacific unless he made an extensive passage down this magnificent arm of the salt sea. He was either in a bay, or among inlets and channels of islands. It mattered little, for he had reached the easternmost shores of the fabled south sea, the goal of all explorers of Canada dating back to the age of Cabot and Cartier. The weather was all in his favor for making preciously important scientific observations—a lon-

gitude and a latitude to place on one of Aaron Arrowsmith's
definitive maps sold in London. He determined to spy out
a place to land and take the necessary measurements.

Now came a new and unexpected problem: native resistance, born of fear, of mistreatment and misunderstanding,
even of ignorance and suspicion. Near what is now called
King Island, Mackenzie met three heavily laden canoes.
The natives in these canoes, possibly Bella Bella, western
neighbors of the Bella Coola, began conversing with the
young natives in Mackenzie's canoe. They picked over the
exploring party's property with an air of disdain and indifference—nothing there seemed of value to these property-
hungry hunters. A past grievance surfaced. One of the natives, in a manner Mackenzie classified as insolent, told that
"a large canoe had lately been in the bay, with people in
her like me, and that one of them, whom he called *Macubah*,
had fired on him and his friends, and that *Bensins* had struck
him on the back, with the flat part of this sword." Another
name was mentioned, unintelligible to Mackenzie. "At the
same time he illustrated these circumstances by the assistance
of my gun and sword; and I do not doubt but he well
deserved the treatment which he described."

Mackenzie wished to be rid of these pests, but before he
could send them packing he had to give up his young guide.
They were flanked by three canoes, and soon at least one
other canoe came from the shore. Mackenzie was ordered
to proceed to a village. They steered to Elcho Bay, and
once ashore he was closely examined. He was told by the
unwelcoming newcomer that "he had been shot at by people
of my colour" and that "Macubah"—Vancouver—had
come there in his large canoe.

The accosting native had been misinformed: Vancouver
was never there in his ship, only in ships' boats. Captain
George Vancouver made no reference to any difficulties
with natives he met in Dean Channel on 2 June. "Bensins"—

the botanist Archibald Menzies—was not a part of any boat expedition. If by "Bensins" the native meant Master James Johnstone, then perhaps there was reason for complaint: Johnstone, leader of a ship's boat, admitted to forcing entrance to a seaside dwelling. No clash with the natives of this quarter is documented in Vancouver's expedition papers. How the natives came to this account is not known. They bore grievances, but these appear to be unfounded or at least undocumented. In any case, Captain Vancouver's men, six weeks and five days earlier, had been examining these same waters as part of his search for the northwest passage. At the time Mackenzie reached this spot, Vancouver was surveying far-off waters that divide present-day British Columbia from Alaska.

The young chief's importunities and anxious movements made it clear to Mackenzie that he was in a hostile land. To this day the place of temporary refuge is disputed territory among natives. The explorer decided to take to an island as the best means of defense; this island is known today as Mackenzie Rock in Sir Alexander Mackenzie Provincial Park. It was overgrown with weeds, and a house and temple stood upon it. Ten canoes pursued Mackenzie and his party. "From their general deportment [wrote the worried expedition leader] I was very apprehensive that some hostile design was meditated against us, and for the first time I acknowledged my apprehensions to my people." He ordered them to be on their guard and be prepared to defend themselves. Mackenzie led the party ashore and took possession of the rock, at the same time making preparations to repel attackers and fight to the last.

Some natives became irksome, and proved to be thieves, carrying away a hat, a handkerchief, and a sounding-line with which Mackenzie took depths of the water. Other natives came to trade and brought a fabulous sea otter skin and a white goat skin. For the former they demanded the impossible—Mackenzie's hanger, or heavy short sword. Mackenzie could not take away with him the bulky goat skin. He sought to drive a hard bargain for the sea otter pelt and concluded that the maritime fur traders had become far too improvident in what they traded for such pelts. The natives constantly replied "No, no" to any offer from the Nor'Wester. Eventually Mackenzie got one of these prize furs, and he may have obtained others as well, as souvenirs— even trophies—of his west coast sojourn. He intended to use them, too, as proof positive that he had reached the Pacific. These sea otter pelts were to become his diplomatic weapon to convince Canadian governors of the promise of transcontinental trade based in Montreal.

At last the party was alone, free from their antagonists. The travelers got a fire going, warmed themselves, fixed a little supper from dwindling rations, and slept as best they could on that rocky bivouac. A two-man watch was posted, and Mackenzie laid himself down on his cloak and gazed at the stars. His mind must have chased down all the channels of yesterday's memories—of his laborious travels and near escapes, of his predicaments past and present. And what would the following day bring?

At eight the next morning, Monday, 22 July, Mackenzie had his instruments at the ready. He took five altitudes for time and after making calculations concluded that his chronometer was slow by one hour, twenty-one minutes, and forty-four seconds. He was now able to make adjustments to his mapping. Mackenzie patiently took a meridian to verify his position. He needed to be sure he had the facts right.

All around the explorer whirled a tumult of natives: people coming and going, bartering and calling, and bringing furs and seal flesh to trade. Mackenzie coolly, stoically declined to stir from his astronomical duties until he had accomplished his object. But he did order his men to get their possessions into the canoe in preparation for a speedy departure. He calculated the latitude of Mackenzie Rock by artificial and natural horizons as being close to what we now know it to be, 52°22'30"N. In subsequent calculations of longitude, Mackenzie placed his position about twenty-five miles too far west—still remarkably close considering his lack of accurate timekeeping with which to check his navigation tables.

The chaos continued to swell. Distractions were required. MacKay got out his burning-glass and soon lighted a fire in the lid of his tobacco-box. This so surprised native observers that they traded their best sea otter skin for the glass. The young chief—"our young Indian"—faithful to the cause of Mackenzie and the expedition, warned that, in Mackenzie's words, these natives "were as numerous as musquitoes, and of very malignant character." The young man worried for his own safety and that of the explorers. With absolute determination Mackenzie had completed his task.

At the last moment, with a degree of foresight that is all the more surprising when we consider his difficulties and the urgent appeals from his men to take evasive action, Mackenzie did what no record of Canadian history ought to fail to record. It is best said in his own understated language:

> I mixed up some vermilion in melted grease, and inscribed, in large characters, on the South-East face of the rock on which we had slept last night, this brief memorial—"Alexander Mackenzie, from Canada, by land, the twenty-second of July, one thousand seven hundred and ninety-three."

Did anyone ever write such a pallid, laconic statement of accomplishment? It was merely a record of who, when, and where. The how and the why are absent from this sentence of such monumental attainment whose significance echoes down through the years.

Nearly a century and a half passed before Captain R. P.

Bishop, a surveyor, believed he had found the actual spot marking the westerly terminus of the amazing journey. When the Canadian government in 1926 placed a monument to this long-neglected and lost historic spot, the prime minister of the day, William Lyon Mackenzie King, sent this message:

> In that simple and inspiring narrative of voyages from Montreal through the continent of North America to the frozen and Pacific oceans Alexander Mackenzie gave the world the first authentic account of the country and revealed the perils and privations of his expeditions. First in a long line of explorers to reach the Pacific by an overland route, he holds an exalted place in world history and his life is a splendid example of the courage, devotion and endurance of the men who laid the foundation of the great heritage we have now the pleasure to enjoy.

Two hundred years after the date Mackenzie made his inscription, a bicentennial celebration of the noteworthy transit took place. At its culmination Arthur Hans, a Bella Coola hereditary chief, presented a university student costumed as Mackenzie, and representing twenty-five Lakehead University "voyageurs" under the leadership of their redoubtable professor, Dr. Jim Smithers, with the eagle down ceremony as a symbol of peace and friendship. The Canadian warship HMCS *Mackenzie* lay in the offing. The Carrier-Chilcotin Tribal Council, whose forbears had assisted Alexander Mackenzie and his party, denied access to the student expedition along the provincially designated heritage trail, over which they claimed exclusive control. The students avoided an altercation by trucking their canoes from the Fraser River to the Pacific. They then paddled the saltwater fjords to Mackenzie Rock, encouraged by Nuxalk hereditary chiefs and their families at the commemorative bicentennial ceremony.

At Dean Channel Mackenzie was treated as a spirit. Oral evidence, saved for the historical record by good fortune, provides a window on a scene for which there is no other native recounting. When Alexander Mackenzie faced native resistance at Mackenzie Rock, as we now know from native testimony gathered by local resident B. F. Jacobsen in the 1940s, he and his men were looked on as raiders. This was natural to these peoples, for they viewed all outsiders as warriors. The natives had prepared to do battle against Mackenzie's party. The "man in the middle looked like a goat," recounted a Bella Bella by the name of Au Kvalla, whose grandfather said he had witnessed Mackenzie's arrival. The natives thought Mackenzie had white paint on his face, it was so pale. Because of his strange appearance, they thought that this visitor must be a spirit. Mackenzie, they noted, had strangely stood up in his canoe. He had moved his arms about. Then at times wonderful stars, or eyes, seemed to shine forth from his person (his sextant was giving off reflections). Soon the spirit sat down and the canoe moved on. The natives then went to the spot and noticed the writing on the rock, which to them looked like crows' marks. The natives could not understand this writing, whose figures, unlike their own, did not resemble animals. Puzzled, they hurried away to their small village of Eaststam to tell their chief about the writing. The chief told them to stay away from the writing, as it might displease their gods.

Mackenzie, meanwhile, had made his departure as quickly and conveniently as he could. He sought safety in a small cove, just west of Cape McKay at the entrance to Cascade Inlet, where on a point of land he and his men landed. He would like to have sounded the depths of the sea in that place, but the natives had "stolen from us . . . a sounding-line." The land around him rose three to seven hundred feet above high-water mark, and Mackenzie stated drily that most likely he would not have been able to plumb the bottom. Where soil existed, huge trees—cedar, spruce-firs, white birch, and others—grew. And from the precipices streams of fine water, cold as ice, came down the rocky face. Here Mackenzie completed his observations, which are recorded in his *Voyages from Montreal*. He felt he had achieved his scientific goal: "I had now determined my situation, which is the most fortunate circumstance of my long, painful, and perilous journey, as a few cloudy days would have prevented me from ascertaining the final longitude of it." In a long footnote, he chided Meares for his rash idea that there existed a practical northwest passage south of 69°50′ "as I flatter myself had been proved by my former voyage [by the Mackenzie River]." To this he added, with complete knowledge of the voyage literature and coast history of English and American navigators:

> Nor can I refrain from expressing my surprise at his [Meares's] assertion, that there was an inland sea or archipelago of great extent between the islands of Nootka and the main, about the latitude where I was at this time. Indeed I have been informed that Captain Grey [Robert Gray], who commanded an American vessel, and on whose authority he ventured this opinion, denies that he had given Mr. Meares any such information. Besides, the contrary is indubitably proved by Captain Vancouver's survey, from which no appeal can me made.

These reflections Mackenzie made in the safety of his study. But out on the shore of the Pacific he had only one thing on his mind—to get those precious observations safely recorded for geographical science. Thus, with his record of transcontinental travel completed, he gave the final general form to North America in those latitudes where, over the course of centuries, geographical speculators had placed straits, bays, passages, seas of the west, and other apocryphal waterways.

The next task was to get home as soon as possible and

to extricate himself from potentially hazardous circumstances in the wilderness. Mackenzie and his party returned the way they had come, and the paddlers kept up a good pace. "Though the tide was running out very strong," he said, "by keeping close in with the rocks, we proceeded at a considerable rate, as my people were very anxious to get out of the reach of the inhabitants of this coast." They paddled all night, it seems, and passed their old encampment at Porcupine Cove. They continued onward, past a well-armed canoe, which sped after them and then stopped and lingered to watch the wayfarers pass. A white-headed eagle soared overhead.

Following advice from his guide, Mackenzie steered for Gom Goltes, a village on the south side of the Bella Coola River. Here Sears Kille, the chief, decided to give a reception for Mackenzie and with it a *Gin-a-ko-mek,* or "dance," the greatest honor they could bestow on anyone. For this event the natives all wore headdresses and prepared to shake eagle down to fall upon the explorer. According to their oral history, the natives approached Mackenzie but, fearing their advance, he took flight. "The chief was very much hurt and somewhat disgusted when the white man left in this manner."

The native testimony does not accord with Mackenzie's narrative, which presents an altogether different account of proceedings. As Mackenzie related the encounter, he stood alone and was met by dagger-carrying natives. Mackenzie raised his gun, then drew his sword. The natives surrounded him, and one tried to pin his arms from the rear, but Mackenzie threw him off. One of Mackenzie's men then arrived, and within ten minutes the rest of the party was there. They loaded and primed their muskets and pistols, drew up in military array before the great houses, and demanded a parley. The young chief then told Mackenzie that the rascal who had made such a nuisance of himself at Dean Channel had been the source of the problem. Evidently he had told the villagers that Mackenzie had ill-treated him and had murdered four of his companions. Mackenzie, seeking to contain his temper, explained the falsehoods. He demanded return of some stolen items, as well as a necessary supply of fish. Eventually restitution was made and the dried fish delivered. Thereafter, Mackenzie referred to the place as Rascal's Village. They bought salmon and then made for the canoe to begin the long, arduous upstream journey. The "rascal," however, had made his way upstream. The Canadians and an Indian, fearing an ambush, refused to embark in the canoe. Instead they took to the riverbanks, leaving Mackenzie and MacKay to pole the canoe. Nothing else in all the journey was as arduous as this, and the canoe, poled alternately by the two men, progressed upstream foot by weary foot. Mackenzie showed some of his finest qualities that day, refusing to be stampeded by his frightened men. Two well-manned canoes came down the river toward them, and there was again fear of death. Happily, the vessels passed on, and that evening the party camped, then pushed on again at first light. Thus did they proceed for a while up this fast flowing stream. They came eventually to that first riverside village where they had been so well received. However, the chief's son had died of the effects of an ulcer, and as a result the chief was angry with Mackenzie, who had attempted to treat the condition. Mackenzie sought to mollify the chief. He gave as much property as he could, including cloths and knives, to the chief's other son, who had gone with him as a guide. A feast ended these difficulties, and eventually the natives gave the travelers a grand sendoff.

Again they were on the trail, with the land of saltwater canoes behind them. Through stately cedars they trudged, and by good fortune met up with the expedition's dog, who had gone missing in the Indian villages. The natives told them that the animal had howled nightly for his absent masters. "Our dog" had become terribly deranged, weary, and famished. The explorers dropped scraps of food along the way to encourage the dog, who eventually ceased his wanderings, again recognizing Mackenzie and party as friends. The mascot rejoined the expedition.

Next they came to Friendly Village, home of the great chief Soocomlick. The natives supplied the travelers with a large quantity of salmon, and the party continued on their journey, now accompanied by a throng of well-wishers. They faced once again those physical hardships that had greeted them all along, through forests, across rivers, and over mountains. Behind them on the trail remained the hazards of memory, the toils of rushing water, the armed threats and retaliations of a violent frontier. Mackenzie's heroism did not go unnoticed. In the early twentieth century a descendant of Soocomlick, one Skimillick, recalled Mackenzie's arrival from over the mountains. Skimillick referred to him as the great White Chief and told how, when Mackenzie's "slaves" were fainthearted, the explorer had put a great shame upon them by doing easily what they found so hard to do. As late as the 1970s Mackenzie's arrival among the Bella Coola remained the stuff of legend. "The chief put a feather on Mackenzie's head to guide him. They spread the contents of his chamber-pot on the trail, before and after him. They thought that he had returned from the dead, so this would prevent him from disappearing."

Getting out of the valley posed a problem, for the party had to scale several thousand vertical feet of cliffs. That evening, after an exhausting ascent, they pondered their deliverance from an environment that could have engulfed them. They sat around the blazing fire and talked of past dangers. They indulged themselves in "the delightful reflection that we were thus far advanced on our homeward journey." Sublime scenery surrounded them. Mackenzie rhapsodized: "Such was the depth of the precipices below, and the height of the mountains above, with the rude and wild magnificence of the scenery around that I shall not attempt to describe such an astonishing and awful combination of objects, of which indeed no description can convey an adequate idea."

The next morning they were on the trail against the rising sun, and for days on end, with frost underfoot, they kept moving. On 28 July they were back at their campsite at Tanya Lakes, their campsite of 16 July. They dug up their pemmican cache and carried on, not meeting a single person on their way, for the natives had apparently gone to the Great River, the Fraser. On the afternoon of 4 August they were back at the banks of the Fraser. There they found their old canoe and their goods untouched. Natives soon gathered around them, and some thefts occurred. Mackenzie threatened retaliatory measures, warning the natives that he would issue orders to prevent salmon from coming up their river. The Pacific belonged to the white man, he said. The natives promptly returned the stolen goods, every last item.

The men loaded the canoe again. They were in high spirits on a river teeming with returning salmon. The party navigated upstream, via McGregor River and Herrick Creek, through mountain portals resembling enormous Gothic churches. They crossed the swampy carrying place to the Bad River and skirted boulders and logjams until at last, on 15 August, they camped on the spot "where some of us had nearly taken our eternal voyage on June 13th." The men's legs and feet were so numb from the cold that Mackenzie worried that they would never survive. They searched in the stream for their bag of lost bullets but went away empty-handed. And then, at last, they reached the Great Divide.

Mackenzie's ankles were now terribly swollen, and in places he had to be carried. In fact, he crossed the continental divide on the arms of others. At the Parsnip River he got into the canoe and that evening glided peacefully down the stream. On 18 August the party's progress was so rapid that they covered in one day a distance that had taken them a week going upriver. Soon they were past Finlay Forks and its rapids, and soon they passed Rocky Mountain Canyon, near Hudson's Hope. Once they were out of the mountains the vistas seemed to open, and soon they could see grazing animals of every description. The hunters made easy targets of elk and bear, and the party and "our dog" ate like gluttons.

The passage downstream on the Peace toward Fort Fork was a voyage of triumph. The western odyssey's next-to-last morning found the argonauts paddling before daylight. When the sun rose, a beautiful country greeted them. They shot a buffalo and bear that day, but discarded them as insufficiently fat to satisfy such fastidious appetites. Before long they were approaching Fort Fork. On 24 August the travelers reached that place by four in the afternoon. They found McLeod and five men doing a routine summertime duty, building a new house.

Mackenzie showed no excitement in his journal. Perhaps exhaustion had taken its toll. In his record for that day, Saturday 24 August, Mackenzie wrote: "At length, as we rounded a point, and came in view of the Fort, we threw out our flag, and accompanied it with a general discharge of our fire-arms; while the men were in such spirits, and made such an active use of their paddles, that we arrived before the two men whom we left here in the spring, could recover their senses to answer us. Thus we landed at four in the afternoon, at the place we had left on the ninth of May."

Mackenzie did not record how he ate that evening, or if he celebrated his return and reunion with his native family, who may have been there or at Fort Chipewyan. He is annoyingly silent on such private matters. He had been absent 108 days, 75 on the way to the Pacific and 33 on return east. From his advance base, Fort Fork on the Peace, he had logged in 74 days about 1,200 miles, 940 through its waterways and 260 backpacking. His average day's travel was about 20 miles. On the return passage, from Friendly Village to the Fraser he had averaged 25 miles a day, and by waterways back from the Fraser to Fort Fork he made 860 miles in 24 days, an average of 36 miles a day. We can only wish that his fellow travelers had saved a few scraps of memoir of their great accomplishments. Doubtless MacKay and others would have made a few references to Mackenzie's hard-driving, unmerciful behavior. No such testimony survives, however. Mackenzie's own narrative is not brightened by even a glint of humor. But as a record of adventure it stands comparison with any account.

Mackenzie had a clear understanding of his achievement. "Here my voyages of discovery terminate," he wrote with frank understatement of the end of his career as explorer.

> Their toils and their dangers, their solicitudes and sufferings, have not been exaggerated in my description. On the contrary, in many instances, language has failed me in the attempt to describe them. I received, however, the reward of my labours, for they were crowned with success.

He had reached no Russian factory and had made no embassy to Czarina Catherine. However, he had brilliantly realized Pond's dream of reaching the Pacific—and by so doing had realized that older, more cherished dream of crossing the continent at its greatest width, thus linking Atlantic to Pacific. His labors were indeed crowned with success. He now resumed the more prosaic character of trader.

CHAPTER 6

Schemes and Dreams

ELEVEN months after he had set forth from Fort Chipewyan on his second great journey, Mackenzie returned to base, his voyage to the Pacific completed. Now only the numerous demands of the fur trade in his department could keep him from pressing eastward out of the Northwest. That winter of 1793–94 found Mackenzie again in difficulty, this time of a different sort than produced by the toil of wilderness travel.

At Fort Chipewyan he remained lodged deep in the Athabasca fur domain. The previous year's exploits across the Rockies and back had taken their toll. On 13 January 1794 he confided to his cousin Roderick his urgent wish that they both could get down to Grand Portage. "I am fully bent on going down," he wrote, with telling signs of frustration at his idleness and exile. "I am more anxious now than ever. For I think it unpardonable in any man to remain in this country who can afford to leave it. What a pretty situation I am in this winter—starving and alone—without the power of doing myself or any body else any Service. The Boy at Lac La Loche or even my own Servant is equal to the performance of my Winter Employment." The hours grew longer in indolence. Mackenzie yearned for relief from inactivity.

In the spring, as soon as conveniently possible, Mackenzie quit Athabasca. He was never to return and had, quite firmly, no intention of doing so. He went first to Grand Portage and the annual meeting of the North West Company partners. There he was voted an additional share in the concern. More important, he was made one of the company's agents. Now Mackenzie could conduct his business in Montreal, and he could engage in the diplomacy of the fur business as far as the constraints of the company and of common sense allowed.

Some of his fellow partners at least recognized his brilliance and accepted his new status as spokesman and "fixer" for their interior commercial affairs. Mackenzie had now crossed a divide in the fur business: he was empowered to represent the "wintering partners" in the higher echelons of the firm. The "interior" traders had long complained that "head office" paid little attention to their needs. By naming Mackenzie agent they hoped to gain a stronger hand in the affairs at Montreal and London and a stronger voice in the councils of the North West Company. They were not disappointed. Even so, the internal struggles in which Mackenzie took a leading part were not resolved until 1804. In the interim many of the traders had good reason to hate Mackenzie. At present, however, all that lay in the future.

For the moment Mackenzie concentrated on informing persons in high places of his findings. His dreams and schemes now flooded from his pen—first as brief notes and letters often requested by officials, then as detailed memoranda, invariably prepared for presentation to those who formulated state business policy in London. Sometime that winter, if not before, he concluded that he had to convince those in power of the merits of his commercial scheme for a new northern empire of commerce. He determined to call on the closest available representative of King George III. This required a detour on his way to Montreal, but it was an important move in his search for patrons and allies. Late summer of 1794 found Mackenzie knocking on the door of the headquarters of the lieutenant governor of the province of Upper Canada, Major John Graves Simcoe. The headquarters, known as Navy Hall, was at Niagara on the Lake, hard by the U.S. boundary and under the guns of Fort Niagara, which was still in British possession. Chosen by Simcoe two years before for his temporary capital, this renovated log building was the residence of Simcoe and his wife, Elizabeth Gwillim Simcoe. At Navy Hall all the administrative business of the fledgling colony was transacted. Here, in as much viceregal splendor as could be arranged, Major and Mrs. Simcoe listened to the explorer recount his tale. Just as on earlier occasions they had taken note of other men's dreams and aspirations—Loyalist refugees, soldiers and sailors, travelers and petitioners—for a stronger British Empire in North America, so did they now interest themselves in what the young and weather-beaten Scot had to tell them.

The refined and cultivated Mrs. Simcoe, in her diary entry for Monday 8 September, gave a good portrait of Mackenzie and his intentions, one that is worth quoting in full:

Mr. Mackenzie, who has made his way from the Grand Portage to the Pacific Ocean, is just returned from thence, and brought the Governor a sea otter skin as a proof of his having reached that coast. He says the savages spear them from the rocks, as the Indians here do sturgeon. These animals are amphibious, but [live] generally in the sea. Mr. McKenzie went down the River of Peace near two degrees north of Lake Superior, and came to the Rocky Mountains, on which rise some rivers that fall into the Atlantic, and others which empty themselves into the Pacific Ocean. He went down a river which falls into the latter and rises not 700 yards from the River of Peace. He afterwards travelled 17 days by land. There are a kind of large sheep on the Rocky mountains, their horns the size of a cow's. The Indians near the coast live on fish, which they are very dexterous in catching; they dry salmon in boxes of a kind of upper story in their huts. They prepare the roes, beating them up with sorrel, a plant with acid taste, till it becomes a kind of caviare, and, when the salmon are dried, boil and mix them with oil. These savages never taste meat, and think if any was thrown into the river the fish would go away. One of Mr. McKenzie's men having thrown the bone of a deer in the water, an Indian dived and fetched it out; nor would they suffer water to be ladled out in a kettle in which meat had been boiled. Are these not veritable fish eaters? Mr McKenzie observed those Indians who inhabited the islands on the coast to be more savage than the others. The otter skins are sold at a great price, by those who trade on the coast, to the Chinese.

Governor Simcoe, who like Alexander Mackenzie was lively and energetic, also danced to the imperial rhythm. Out of this wilderness of forests Simcoe intended in patriarchal fashion to establish a society of industrious loyal subjects free from republicanism. Much of his administrative activity was devoted to the military security of this fledgling western-most settlement of the British Empire in America. That involved conducting successful relations with native peoples of his province and stimulating commerce, including the trade in furs.

What Mackenzie told the governor was not lost on this empire builder. In his subsequent dispatch to that British government body charged with setting trade strategy and regulations, known augustly as the Committee of the Privy Council for Trade and Foreign Plantations to the House of Lords, Simcoe reported the conversation in detail. This first statement of Mackenzie's intent is the prototype of a message Mackenzie was to preach in season and out of season to all who would listen. The essence of the concept was as follows:

He [Mackenzie] describes the communications between Upper Canada & this Ocean [the Pacific] to be practicable, similar methods being pursued by which the Northwest Company have already extended their factories over the internal parts of the Country, the height of the land between the Peace River which he ascended to its source & branches of the great River, which he supposes to be the River of the West, not being more than seven hundred yards.

Simcoe applauded Mackenzie, saying that he was "as intelligent as he is adventurous." Simcoe continued: "[T]o carry this Commerce to National Advantages, the privileges & rivalship, the claims & monopoly of great commercial Companies must be reconciled & blended in one common Interest."In commenting on Mackenzie's scheme, he advised:

The Northwest Traders would find it their Interest to collect the most valuable of the Furs, now brought from the interior parts of America, & to pass them down the Streams which fall into the Pacific Ocean—& this Mr. McKenzie says that they could do with less Expense & difficulty than bringing them thro' the St. Laurence. In respect to the valuable furs on the Coast of the Pacific Ocean, his ideas are that a Post at Cookes River & another at the Southerly limit of the British Claims would probably secure the whole Traffic, & as this cannot be done in any other manner than by conciliating the affection of the natives, it is natural to suppose as he is persuaded, that the habits of a people long accustomed to the manners & disposition of the Indians, will be found to be of the greatest consequence to promote so desirable a purpose; the crews of trading Vessels seem by no means fit for this traffic & the Russia[n]s have severely felt their ignorance of its Customs.

By these means, Mackenzie knew, sea otter furs sold into China would hasten the export of hotly sought-after items such as tea, porcelains, and other goods from Canton and elsewhere. Trade to China would flourish, for furs imported would reduce the requirement to bring silver from England and India as "cash" payment for the Chinese. A brief report of Mackenzie's travels, which the explorer penned on 10

September in his rooms in Hind's Tavern in York, now Toronto, reached Simcoe's eager hands a few days later. Soon that document became the evidence that Lieutenant Governor Simcoe in Niagara and, in turn, Governor Dorchester in Montreal employed to pressure the British government into understanding Mackenzie's achievement. Not only had the continent been crossed overland in northern latitudes by a British subject, but also an enlarged field of commerce awaited Canadian and British traders—provided that certain problems could be surmounted.

In Montreal Mackenzie lay ill for a time, and he was denied the satisfaction of visiting Lord Dorchester. Circumstances now compelled him to go to England by way of the United States, probably via New York or Philadelphia. On the way to London Mackenzie surely promoted his business concerns to any trusted associates he encountered, for that was his custom.

We do not know why Mackenzie was unable to see Lord Dorchester. In any case, his journal stood in a state of general disorder, and if the truth be told, his mind was similarly circumstanced. Before leaving Athabasca for the St. Lawrence area he had written to ever loyal confidant Roderick Mackenzie to explain that he had begun the task of copying the journal. His progress stalled. His mind wandered. "The greatest part of my time was taken up in vain Speculations," he confessed. "I got into such a habit of thinking that I was often lost in thoughts nor could I ever write to the purpose." He explained, "What I was thinking of, would often occur to me instead of that which I ought to do. I never passed so much of my time insignificantly, nor so uneasy." What flashed across his mind can only be imagined. He put it this way: "Although I am not superstitious, dreams amongst other things, caused me much annoyance. I could not close my eyes without finding myself in company with the Dead.

I had some visions of late which almost convinced me that I lost a near relation or a friend." Mackenzie's mind was never at ease, and he was unable to do anything about it. Mental illness? Perhaps. Certainly he was exhausted, and he could neither write nor edit. Instead he put his manuscript aside, expecting to undertake the work more speedily once good health returned. Like many another writer he was to find the task more challenging than ever anticipated, and the huge size of his eventually published book indicates the immensity of the task that lay before him at this stage of his life. Doubtless, Mackenzie had been very ill, even delirious. By late July he felt better and could write to friends that he was "a great deal recovered from my indisposition, my greatest ailing is the remainder of a stitch which affected my left breast passing the [Grand] Portage." He may have suffered a minor heart attack.

Travel to New York, to catch the next boat, and to London, to do further business, offered new horizons for wilderness-weary Mackenzie, and provided relief from frontier trading and from the petulant dealings in the counting-houses of Montreal. New York was already the headquarters of a cluster of merchants doing business in Macao and Canton. Here the pulse of international commerce was strong, seaborne trade flourished, and speculators resumed older occupations set aside during the revolutionary war. In New York and Philadelphia John Ledyard, who had sailed with James Cook on his 1778 voyage to Nootka and Alaska, had peddled recently his plan to open up American trade with China. From New York the *Empress of China*, financed by Philadelphia merchants, sailed to initiate American trade with the Chinese, and returned in 1785 with a full lading of teas, porcelain, silk, and other exotic goods. It was, Ledyard said, "the greatest commercial enterprise that has ever been embarked on in this country." Mackenzie and Ledyard were two of a kind, and it would be fascinating to know if these "fixers" ever got together over a noggin to plot trade strategy.

We do not know exactly when or how Mackenzie spent his time in New York. In that year, 1794, he soon became aware, if he did not know already, that the Nor'Westers could use the U.S. trading connection with China to sell their furs in the Orient. In 1792, two years before Mackenzie confided his scheme to Governor Simcoe, the partnership of McTavish, Frobisher and Alexander Henry, and possibly John Jacob Astor, had chartered two ships, the *Washington* and the *America,* to convey pelts to China by way of Cape Horn. The return cargo of yard goods, tea, and semi-porcelain purchased in Canton had been sold to Astor. This direct and profitable Canadian venture to China was followed by a second, more ambitious undertaking that involved the conveyance of 4,000 beaver pelts and was undertaken by an 800-ton vessel chartered in New York.

This trade gained impetus when Mackenzie, now a principal partner in the concern of McTavish, Frobisher and associates, a powerful agency within the North West Company, began to implement his plan. Mackenzie believed that the future—even the salvation—of the northwest fur trade lay in access to the Pacific, in embracing and engulfing all Hudson's Bay Company monopoly rights, and in developing whatever arrangements with the Americans were required to get a direct trade to China. As time passed he became increasingly convinced that the Americans were only a means of convenience and that ultimately there would be no collaboration with them. In 1798, having convinced his partners to extend their capital outlay, Mackenzie once again journeyed to New York. There he purchased in the name of William Seton and William Magee Seton, both citizens of the United States and residents of New York, the 340-ton ship *Northern Liberties.* He had her coppered and fitted out.

He also convinced Messrs. Seton, Maitland & Co. of New York to invest $25,000 in the project. For some years, until 1804, this remained an annual arrangement, and for a while Philadelphia merchants Messrs. Nicklin and Griffiths were involved in a parallel arrangement with the Montreal concern. The Mackenzie interest invested mightily in the *Northern Liberties* venture, including $25,000 in the ship, $10,000 in the outfit (guns, provisions, and two months' wages advanced to the men involved), $40,000 in specie (to pay to the Chinese), and another $40,000 in furs. Mackenzie had the venture insured for the total cost, that is, $125,000, and for the duration of the intended voyage from New York to Canton and thence to any European port, with leave to call at Falmouth, England, for "orders warranted American property." Thus was the subterfuge of using foreign cargo ships complete.

The success of this voyage encouraged the Nor'Westers to consign further furs of first quality to China. Regrettably, however, the company lacked sufficient numbers of first-quality pelts for both its London and its Canton markets; in consequence, the London trade began to suffer, much to the regret of the London partners. Thus the Montreal interests of the North West Company were soon at odds with their London counterparts. The "Canadians" wanted to extend the new field of Asian commerce, while the "British" associates warned that the Canton enterprise would weaken their position on the London market in relation to the Hudson's Bay Company, to say nothing of running afoul of East India Company regulations and French warships at large on the high seas.

To Mackenzie's way of advanced thinking, Canton commanded the day. This actual extension of markets tied in naturally with his strategy of enlarging, with deliberate speed, company trade across North America. Athabasca was the farthest western point from which furs could, with profit, be sent east to Montreal and then to markets. Why not send the Athabasca returns westward to the Pacific? Here was the origin of what later became known in North West Company circles as "the Columbian enterprise." At this germinal stage Mackenzie was pressing for a division of company exports: On the one hand, pelts could be sent via Hudson Bay (thus avoiding the expensive Montreal route); on the other, western furs would be taken to the Pacific, where company ships would transport them to China ports.

Mackenzie also thought in global terms of how he could outflank the East India, South Sea, and Hudson's Bay Companies. All of them, it seemed, had monopoly advantages that lay across the course of Nor'Wester destiny. Together they were a deadly opposition to him. He too needed monopoly protection. He reasoned, and rightly, that the fishery of the North Pacific offered a field of commerce of immense possibility. He aimed to diversify the trade of the Pacific Coast, which at that time consisted primarily of the trade in sea otter skins. He planned to set up a new firm called The Fishery and Fur Company. Whaling ships would take trade items to the northwest coast. An entrepôt of trade and an organizational center would be built at Nootka Sound, with smaller posts on the Columbia River in the south and at Sea Otter Harbour in the north, in latitude 55°. Mackenzie laid his plan before the secretary of state for war and the colonies, Lord Hobart, in January 1802, under the grand title of "Preliminaries to the Establishment of a permanent Fishery & Trade in Furs &c. in the interior and on the West Coast of North America." Eight months later Mackenzie again appealed to the Colonial Office for support. This time he added a strategic issue to the commercial arguments and called for military protection, the building of an establishment on the northwest coast, and the means of forestalling foreign rivals.

At this stage, Mackenzie encountered the greatest opposition not from government nor perhaps from the chartered companies, but from certain Montreal interests. For the past ten or fifteen years, even during his two expeditions, Mackenzie had been at odds with business partners as well as opponents in Canada. When Simon McTavish in 1796 advanced his nephew William McGillivray in preference to Mackenzie, despite the backing of influential wintering partners, Mackenzie became angry. He "went off in a pet," observed Alexander Henry the Elder with relish, "the case as far as I can learn was who should be first—McTavish or McK—and as there could not be two Caesars in Rome one must remove."

The immediate origins of this struggle date from 1799. The agreement, or terms of association, of the North West Company was due to expire in that year. The complications of forging a new deal among pesky partners, some benign, others flamboyantly aggressive, gave Mackenzie the opportunity for commanding independence that he had long sought. He chafed at the old, tyrannical inactivity that was forced upon him by others in the concern. Above all, he hated the domination of McTavish. Mackenzie did not control sufficient voting shares. But if alliances could occur among the Montreal houses and agencies, so could divorces. Out of such disputes arose in 1800 the New North West Company, which, like its powerful and more seasoned rival, was a federation of countinghouses. But in its infancy the new company was feeble and feckless. Expected supporters did not rally to Mackenzie. "You may remember the powers Sir Alexander Mackenzie was possessed of when he made the break with Simon McTavish," one veteran recounted to another, "but not one of them joined the standard of the Knight."

Even so, Alexander Mackenzie had become his own premier at last. The New North West Company is best known in the journals of the wintering partners of the North West

Company as the XY Company. The likeliest origin for this name is the fact that its trade bales bore the markings *X* and *Y*—following on, as it were, from the *N* and *W* designations on the Nor'Westers' bales. Rivals derisively called the new firm's men the "little Potties" (a corruption of *les petits*). Mackenzie may have gone off in a pet, as Henry remarked, but all indications showed that he intended revenge against former allies of the trade based upon Montreal. Along the northwestern trap lines and in adjacent frontier posts, a Canadian fur war now waged, of a bitterness hitherto unseen in the trade. Before long the rivalry between the old and new Nor'Westers grew to violent proportions, strangely presaging a greater battle against the Hudson's Bay Company in later years. New forts were thrown up, and liquor and arms were imported in greater volume. All Mackenzie said in his published travels, in 1801, was that it remained to be decided whether two parties of different size and strength could carry on the struggle, or if there would have to be a merger.

Mackenzie's antagonism toward others even extended to his trusty cousin Roderick. When Alexander quit the North West Company in 1799 to form the XY Company, Roderick was made partner in his place. Coolness descended on the relationship, which only warmed after the 1804 amalgamation.

In a way, Mackenzie was himself the root of the problem, the determined opponent of the larger concern. Doubtless he was resented in certain quarters of Montreal and of London besides, and everywhere he must have been watched with suspicion, even with envy. But his relentless pressures on government—almost a one-man campaign that he spearheaded for trading allies in Canada—had one signal result, an important step in Canadian constitutional history. This related to the crucial matter of peace on the frontier, which Captain Brehm at Michilimackinac had been appealing for at the time Mackenzie embarked upon his trade in the Indian Territories.

Government had been alerted to the bitter hostility between the two companies, a rivalry carried on "with a Jealousy and Rancour improper to the Subjects of the same Empire." Natives had been led to pillage canoes, retaliation had become customary, force prevailed over justice. The fur trade would come to an end if government failed to establish a competent jurisdiction in the Canadian provinces for investigation of crimes committed in the British Indian Territories that lay west and north of the limits of the settled colonies. Other calls came for an extension of imperial law, and thus was born, on the basis of representations made by Mackenzie, the legislation that gave western Canada its first judicial system. In 1803 an act was passed giving Canadian courts jurisdiction over the Indian Territory.

Mackenzie had told Lord Hobart that a coalition between the North West Company and the XY Company would be necessary to achieve the desired end. As he anticipated, his scheme for uniting the concerns met resistance from "the Premier," Simon McTavish, who did not want his own preeminent role and that of Montreal reduced. There the situation remained. With McTavish's death in 1804 and the rise of his nephew William McGillivray to a position of authority in the reorganized firm of McTavish, McGillivray and Company, conditions became more propitious for implementing Mackenzie's scheme. Although Mackenzie became a shareholding giant in the amalgamation, he was deliberately "excluded from any interference." "With him and McGillivray," wrote an influential Montrealer, "there will, I fear, never be intimacy."

Mackenzie, with characteristic restlessness, now sought new worlds to conquer. Denied the opportunity to fix the affairs of the Montreal trade to the Northwest, he was at least free to return to his interests in the Great Lakes and

New York. In 1806 Mackenzie and his associates formed the Michilimackinac Fur Company. Their intention, as we might imagine, was to forestall the expansion of the New York trader John Jacob Astor in the Old Northwest. The rise of Astor's larger intentions of trade to the Pacific alarmed the Nor'Westers, for they did not wish to see their Columbia enterprise preempted. Indeed, in 1809 they rejected Astor's offer that the Canadians purchase one-third of the stock in his Pacific plan. They preferred to go it alone. However, five disgruntled Nor'Westers, including Mackenzie's trusty lieutenant Alexander MacKay, dissatisfied with the company reorganization of 1804, fell in with Astor. They were included in the Pacific Fur Company agreement of June 1810. Thus was born the great American company that sent the *Tonquin* to the mouth of the Columbia River (arrived 22 March 1811), built a marine depot and post called Astoria, and forestalled the Nor'Westers at the mouth of the Columbia River.

Meanwhile, Mackenzie remained an uneasy partner in the Canadian fur trade. He seems to have remained continually outraged by superiors and by business associates, who similarly must have found him a constant source of aggravation. In 1799 Mackenzie could not come to an understanding with his Montreal associates, and his engagement by the North West Company expired. Roderick maintained that this was owing to a misunderstanding. But Alexander was undeniably a difficult individual. The circumstances of the renewal as offered must not have suited him, and if he could not have it to his advantage he would not have it at all. Accordingly, as his cousin put it, "he announced at the first general meeting of Partners at the Grand Portage that, feeling himself uncomfortable, he could not think of renewing his engagements and was determined to withdraw from the Concern."

Mackenzie's announcement brought on a serious discussion, for the wintering partners stated that they could not carry on without him. They even went on record, by a resolution unanimously passed, that "Mr. MacKenzie, having their sole confidence, they could not dispense with his services, therefore that every means should be adopted to retain him." This we have from the records of his cousin. No firm statement of confidence and support, however, could win Mackenzie's favor. "[U]nfortunately," remarks Roderick, "the best endeavours of his friends were of no avail, for he retired in November and crossed the Atlantic."

First Mackenzie settled all his arrangements at Grand Portage and sent a sheaf of letters and instructions to partners and clerks concerning the forthcoming season's obligations and requirements. Then he said goodbye to Grand Portage, and on 17 August 1799 he sailed for Sault Ste. Marie, which he reached five days later. "I expect in ten days hence God willith to dine with my Friends in Montreal," he told a friend.

By late October he was in and out of Montreal and then outward bound from Quebec for England aboard the ship *Desire*. "Although we have been more fortunate in our voyage from Quebec than you and I were in our trip from Montreal to there," he wrote his cousin in Canada, "I have frequently reflected on the situation I left you in after experiencing so much fatigue, and upon other matters not less serious." The previous winter's toil had taken its toll; Mackenzie was exhausted by work, even fretful of arrangements. He had quit the upper country in a hurry and boarded the first outward-bound ship without having attended to legal matters. Now, as he sailed the North Atlantic toward England, his mind filled with problems of unfinished business. He thus sent his cousin Roderick a power of attorney and instructed him to open all letters from "the Upper Province" (the Northwest) and write replies as needed. He was to send fifty pounds to "Mrs. Mackenzie of Three Rivers," a lady

whose relationship to Alexander is not precisely known, but
who may have been one of his aunts. Alexander Mackenzie
had other family obligations as well. Roderick was for awhile
to make a similar payment each year to "Kitty," presumably
his native wife The Catt at Fort Chipewyan. Alexander explained:

> This sum I mean to continue to her annually while Kitty remains
> Single, and if I find that it is not sufficient with the support
> afforded her by her other friends I can easily augment and
> continue it as long as I please. That young woman they have
> taken to their House [Fort Chipewyan] must be in want of
> many necessaries to appear decently. Will you send her ten
> Pounds on my account. This is only a hundredth part of what
> I mean to spend annually, that is one Thousand a year, which
> I can well afford.

And further: "There are a few trifling claims upon me which
I [wish to be] satisfied. If you will go to the Upper Province,
Get Twenty five pounds to give to my aunt."

There is an air of impending finality to this letter, a solemn
hint that Alexander, fatigued and ailing, desired to settle
accounts and provide for survivors of his estate. In fact, both
recovery and surprises lay ahead. In Canada he had become
acquainted with Prince Edward, duke of Kent, a son of King
George III and later father of Queen Victoria. They were
close friends and traveling companions. Both were known
to Simcoe, Lord Dorchester, and other governors of Canada. Both frequented The Beaver Club, a dining society of
the fur trade plutocracy in Montreal. The duke must have
recommended Alexander for public recognition, or perhaps
by now he had become well known in London circles for
his magnificent discoveries.

In any event, it was Mackenzie's famous book that
brought him immediate public acclaim, for in that age travel
books, though expensive, were eagerly consumed by the

reading public. In December 1801 Mackenzie's newly published *Voyages from Montreal* sold briskly at every bookstall
in London. The book contained engraved maps made from
Mackenzie's drawings. The text, based on his journals, memoranda, and notes, had the benefit of an editorial touch-up
by the evenhanded, well-practiced William Coombe, working in confinement in debtor's prison. The publisher of the
book was none other than the superb firm of Cadell and
Davies, leaders in their day. Mackenzie dedicated his book
to King George III; this dedication may have been arranged,
as it had to be, by someone well placed, perhaps Sir Joseph
Banks. With the duke of York's backing, royal attention
was assured. On 10 February 1802 the author became Sir
Alexander Mackenzie, Knight Bachelor.

News of this elevation, previously unknown in Canadian
commercial circles, soon drifted back to Montreal and appeared in Canadian newspapers. Some readers looked on
Mackenzie's rise with envy, others with indifference, and
still others with a touch of mirth. In the latter category was
the wife of Dr. Harry Munro, a surgeon wintering at Fort
William, Lake Superior. Mrs. Munro, living more comfort-
ably in the province of Quebec, instructed her spouse to
"grease your boots & travel up to find the N. West passage
from the North to the South Sea & then you will certainly
come out with the title of Lord Munro Baron of the S.
Sea." Mackenzie's more practical business associates used
his title to good effect to bolster the fortunes of the XY
Company, which now assumed the grander title "Sir Alexander Mackenzie & Co."

In London, among the beaux and belles of society, Sir
Alexander Mackenzie, now fêted and lionized, must have
cut a fine figure. The London Scots, or London Scottish,
were a thriving class of nobles, wealthy landowners, and
traders. In London they gathered for their winter season;
held numerous special dinners, parties, and balls; and devel-

oped a regular round of social life. London drew wealthy Scots like a magnet. In those days, it was said, a farm manager from distant Inverness or Dornoch who wished advice from his laird was obliged to travel to London to find him. London's chief banks, Drummonds among others, were owned and operated by Scots, and shipping and insurance were other fields of opportunity for these North Britons. London was the heart of empire, and Mackenzie fitted into it grandly. Like the composer Felix Mendelssohn-Bartholdy, who affectionately called London "this smoky nest," Mackenzie thrived on its connections and social whirl. In the crowded coffeehouses of the day, like any other businessman, he pored over the papers, checked the shipping lists, and examined the financial notices. His mind must have raced with the necessity of advancing his pet scheme; given his secretive nature, however, it is not likely that he confided in others as to his pet project. He always saved his information for persons in power. Tight-fistedness and secrecy were enduring characteristics of Mackenzie.

Mackenzie thus took his commercial campaign to the seats of power. We can imagine the famous explorer in London streets, lanes, and squares. Of middle age, weatherbeaten, stooped from illness, and old before his time, he may be imagined leaving his house at 38 Norfolk Street, Adelphi, near Chancery Lane and Aldwych. He walks purposefully through byways and thoroughfares toward the Colonial Office, housed in comfortless and decaying houses at 14 Downing Street, hub of the British Empire. Admirably dressed, as befits a wealthy man of his mercantile situation, he has recently sat before the great portrait artist Sir Thomas Lawrence. His knighthood has marked him out in social circles. He has left the rough and tumble of the Canadian wilderness and the easier circumstances of Montreal. Clutching a brief of papers and a copy of his recently published *Voyages from Montreal* under his arm, he prepares to knock on the door of the Colonial Office and lay before an under-secretary the dream of his years. His visit is a minuscule episode in a larger drama, what one fur trade historian called "the old story of relentless competition, demand for freedom from government interference and regulation, and pressure for special privilege through politics and diplomacy." Many had crossed the threshold of the drab Colonial Office, only to be listened to and then turned away. Mackenzie arrived with hope and his appearance was expected.

From Canada, we know, Governors Simcoe and Dorchester had pressed upon their superiors in London, successive secretaries of state for colonial affairs, Mackenzie's ideas for stimulating and redesigning Canadian trade. In London, however, such a plan was met with indifference or even obstruction. The giant Hudson's Bay Company, chartered and wealthy, enjoyed special favor in the circles of profit and power. Still, the appeals came from Upper and Lower Canada. Dorchester, for instance, had attempted to convince his superior, the duke of Portland, that because the Montreal-based traders were so important to the British Empire, it stood to reason that London statesmen ought to know about Mackenzie's discoveries and his brilliant plans. The governor also reported that Mackenzie had determined to proceed to England for the specific purpose of acquainting the minister with particulars of his travels. All of that had passed eight years before, in 1794, and nothing had been done. Convinced that a northwest passage remained only conjecture, Mackenzie had determined to advise government accordingly and to shift the logic to a commercially based scheme that did not depend on such a sea lane.

Mackenzie stood far ahead of his time in this new thinking, and he was a harbinger of the trade reforms of William Huskisson in the 1820s. The Colonial Office still had to listen to the Hudson's Bay Company and its glacial resistance (backed by the precious charter) to any sharing of access to trade by Hudson Bay. At every turn Mackenzie and the Montreal-based entrepreneurs sought relief from the Bay traders' monopoly. They might be able to outtrade their rivals in the *pays d'en haut* and exploit their triumphant ascendancy in Athabasca. Yet the fact remained that unless they could get a guaranteed access through Ruperts Land to Hudson Bay without let or hindrance, they faced expensive transportation of outgoing furs and incoming merchandise. So Mackenzie, at this stage, impatiently faced innumerable corporate obstacles and government regulations.

In the circumstances, Mackenzie redefined his strategy. He attempted to reach agreement with the Hudson's Bay Company through an intermediary, his associate Edward "Bear" Ellice, a key player in the XY Company and a powerful politician in Britain. Mackenzie's idea for solving the problem was to buy out the Hudson's Bay Company, and that is what Ellice proposed in 1803 to the Gentlemen Adventurers on behalf of Mackenzie. The acquisition failed, and so did a rival attempt by the North West Company in 1811.

From its headquarters in the City of London, the Governor and Committee of the Gentlemen Adventurers of England trading into Hudson's Bay watched the activities of Mackenzie with growing concern. They knew of his success in Athabasca and had directed their own explorations there. They knew, too, of his track along the Peace and the northern reaches of the Fraser, and they viewed with dismay and alarm a map that was placed before them, Sir James Winter Lake's "Sketch of Mackenzie's Track along the Rivers Nunijah and Tatouche" (1805). Already Aaron Arrowsmith's quasi-official map of northern North America (1795) showed Mackenzie's routes north and west, outflanking the Bay traders in the Northwest.

Talk circulated, too, of Mackenzie's newfangled scheme

for a bold enterprise to be known as The Fishery and Fur Company. Mackenzie's project, formally presented to the government on 7 January 1802, sat on the desk of the secretary of state for war and the colonies, Lord Hobart. Eight months later Mackenzie made a more urgent appeal, this time requesting a defensible establishment, to be built as part of his west coast bases in order to strengthen claims and forestall foreign rivals.

Mackenzie did not specify whether it was Spain, Russia, France, or the United States that he feared might run up its flag on the west coast of North America. In earlier calls for action he referred to Spanish threats, in later ones to American encroachments. Great Britain was locked in a titanic struggle with Emperor Napoleon, and the possibility of a Spanish, American, or Russian grab at Nootka or elsewhere seemed unlikely for several reasons. Although these were the years of Nelson's great triumphs at sea, such overall naval mastery did not preclude Napoleon from threatening invasion of England. The emperor had a copy of Mackenzie's great book, the only comprehensive guide to Canada's waterways, procured through smugglers and translated into French. Napoleon, with unquenchable thirst for military knowledge, intended to use it as a guide to the rivers of Canada. He believed that French forces landing at New Orleans could do all manner of mischief. They could ascend the Mississippi, cross via the Ohio to the Canadian border lakes, and distract the British by pouncing upon their garrisons in Canada. In the end Napoleon could not use Mackenzie's book as a guide to the military geography of North America: The Russian campaign, recalled Napoleon's adviser Marshal Bernadotte, "knocked that of Canada on the head until Russia was crushed, but it had pleased God to ordain it otherwise." Bernadotte chuckled to think that Canada could have been taken in reverse, from its upper waters, but

he looked upon Mackenzie's great book of travels as a guide
to a military campaign that might have changed the world.
Instead, there had been only defeat and exile.

For his own part, in these years Mackenzie turned increasingly to the question of American incursions on the southern
frontier of Canadian trade. The president of the United
States, the prescient Thomas Jefferson, knew of Mackenzie's
transcontinental journey and comprehended its geopolitical
meaning. For the moment, however, Jefferson still talked
quietly, as many Americans did, of a series of associated
republics that would bring U.S. power to the Pacific; the
concept of a transcontinental United States was not yet fully
formed. For the present, an exploring expedition might
serve the not-too-alarming purposes of showing the flag,
winning native allies, and evaluating the environment. Meriwether Lewis, a captain of infantry, carried Mackenzie's map
westward as a reference and kept an eye out for Mackenzie's
believed Columbia River, "Tacootche-tessee River." Lewis
and Clark's official expedition was a southerly counterpart
of Mackenzie's private voyage and undeniably bolstered
American rights to the Columbia.

Mackenzie, far in advance of the slumbering Colonial
Office, understood the potential American threat as evi-
denced by Lewis and Clark's discoveries and by the U.S.
acquisition of Louisiana in 1803. The first to raise the alarm
about possible loss of the Oregon country through British
indifference, Mackenzie pronounced upon the groundless
nature of U.S. claims and the preeminence of those of the
British. "I myself [am] known to have been the first, who
crossed thro' it to the Columbia, and from the Columbia
[Fraser] to the Pacific Ocean in the year 1793." He claimed
that special privileges ought to be granted to his fur-trading
allies in Canada before the Americans made any further
attempt to seize possession.

In response to Mackenzie's warnings of U.S. designs, the

British cabinet set aside any new claims and did not put the matter at rest in the way the explorer advised. The cabinet argued the opposite, maintaining that any Canadian trade monopoly might infringe on U.S. claims to sovereignty in the Pacific Northwest. Legal opinion, sought by the cabinet, advised against infringing on U.S. territory and thus against granting any exclusive trade privilege to Mackenzie.

With bulldog persistence Mackenzie stuck to his schemes, which changed slightly, as such things were bound to do with the passing of years and the shifting nature of foreign relations. Alive to new, alarming prospects of Astor's brigades penetrating, even subverting, the Montreal-based trade from the south, Mackenzie and his partners in 1806 formed a new firm, the Michilimackinac Fur Company. Their aim was to forestall the Americans in the Old Northwest.

At this stage Mackenzie's commercial strategy assumed protectionist leanings. In 1808 Mackenzie made a renewed attempt on government, this time addressing himself to Viscount Castlereagh, the foreign secretary. This time Mackenzie pressed for an exclusive privilege of commerce in western North America. He now had his heart set on the mouth of the Columbia as the best spot for a Pacific coast anchor of a trading empire. Here an entrepôt could be established for conducting an interior trade as well as trading on the coast. By now he had surmised that the Fraser River stood secondary in importance in trade and navigability to the Columbia.

That River, the Columbia or Oregon, seems designed by Nature, as the Channel of Communication: it being of all the Rivers that empty themselves into the Western Pacific Ocean, the only one capable of being navigated. . . . Its Banks form the first level Country in all the southward Extent of the Continental Coast, from Cooks Entry [Inlet], and consequently the most northern situation on the main Land, that is suited to the residence of a civilized People.

The parent North West Company knew of Astor's intentions but adamantly refused to accept any partnership arrangement for opening the Pacific trade at the mouth of the Columbia.

Not until the United States and Britain commenced hostilities in 1812 did ministers in Whitehall take action to protect northwest coast traders. Otherwise preoccupied with protecting seaborne commerce in places of urgent need, they did not consider it necessary to revert to a discarded plan of an earlier age to put a garrison at Nootka Sound to protect British trade. British government action, when it came, was too late. What Mackenzie had warned of repeatedly for a decade had been achieved by the Americans using the "golden round" of commerce from Europe, eastern North America, the northwest coast and Canton, using the Hawaiian Islands as a winter rendezvous and base. Similarly, by their inaction the British left the door open for American expansion in the Columbia River basin. Half a century before the Oregon crisis ended the issue, the British preferred trade to dominion—but not trade that would get them into trouble with American demands.

While London considered and reconsidered Mackenzie's schemes, and heard representations and appeals from other quarters, Mackenzie returned to Canada in the spring of 1802. Friends in Canada convinced him to stand for election to the Legislative Assembly of Lower Canada for the county of Huntingdon, which he did on 16 June 1804, and in January of the next year he first attended the required sessions in Quebec City. At the outset he enjoyed the varied society of that ancient garrisoned town, with its bustling social whirl, and for a time he thought he had made a good arrangement. Quickly, however, he grew restless. Adulation from his peers failed to suffice. "I feel myself much obliged by the attention I usually receive," he confided to Roderick on 24 January 1805, "and this the Stronger as it is from

Strangers." But legislation bored him and made him heartily tired. "I sincerely wish that those who thought themselves my friends in being the means of getting me to so honorable a situation had been otherwise employed," he grumbled. As for the men of the assembly, he hated their easygoing penchant for taxing the source of colonial wealth, the peltry business: "No tax will go down with them except upon commerce which they have no objection to extend to any sum you like." In order to build jails, the legislature proposed to tax men of the North West Company and to impose heavy duties on furs and peltries. Mackenzie sang the Canadian entrepreneur's credo.

In Quebec and Montreal Mackenzie and his business associates enjoyed the full blush of a colonial-imperial society—one dominated by Scottish entrepreneurs, British army officers and Indian agents, and French advocates and jurists. It was altogether a buoyant community of elites, and Mackenzie took an honored place in it. Surviving records provide occasional glimpses of his renown. For example, Mackenzie and Duncan McGillivray, brother of William McGillivray, hosted a dinner at which one of the guests, the young and wide-eyed George Landmann, lieutenant in the Corps of Engineers, made close observations. "In those days we dined at four o'clock," recorded Landmann,

> and after taking a satisfactory quantity of wine, perhaps a bottle each, the married men, viz, Sir John Johnson, McTavish, Frobisher, O'Brien, Judge Ogden, Tom Walker, and some others retired, leaving about a dozen to drink to their health. We now began in right earnest and true highland style, and by four o'clock in the morning, the whole of us had arrived at such a degree of perfection, that we could all give the war-whoop as well as Mackenzie and McGillivray, we could all sing admirably, we could all drink like fishes, and we all thought we could dance on the table without disturbing a single decanter, glass or plate by which it was profusely covered; but on making the

experiment we discovered that it was a complete delusion, and ultimately, we broke all the plates, glasses, bottles, &c., and the table also, and worse than all the heads and hands of the party received many severe contusions, cuts and scratches.

Here and elsewhere Mackenzie was often the life of the party. Landmann took note of Mackenzie's flamboyant, inebriated behavior. In company with Nor'Westers at Lachine they stopped for a grand picnic, and Landmann, who was English, chuckled that he was the only foreigner among all these Highlanders. "We sat down," he recorded,

> and without loss of time expedited the lunch intended to supersede a dinner, during which time the bottle had freely circulated, raising the old Highland drinking propensity, so that there was no stopping it; Highland speeches and sayings, Highland reminiscences, and Highland farewells, with the dioch and dorich, over and over again, was kept up with extraordinary energy, so that by six or seven o'clock, I had, in common with many of the others fallen from my seat. To save my legs from being trampled on, I contrived to draw myself into the fireplace, and sat up in one of the corners. . . . I there remained very passive, contemplating the proceedings of those who still remained at table, when at length Sir Alexander Mackenzie, as president, and McGillivray, as vice-president, were the last retaining their seats. Mackenzie now proposed to drink to our memory, and then give the war-whoop over us, fallen heroes or friends, all nevertheless on the floor, and in attempting to push the bottle to McGillivray, at the opposite end of the table, he slid off his chair, and could not recover his seat whilst McGillivray, in extending himself over the table, in the hope of seizing the bottle which Mackenzie had attempted to push to him, also in like manner began to slide on one side, and fell helpless on the floor.

At the Beaver Club also, held at the Montreal Hotel and other fancy taverns in those days, such bacchanalia occurred on a regular basis—perhaps every two weeks or so from

December to April. Here honored guests and regular members solemnly drank the five toasts: to the mother of all the saints; to the king; to the fur trade in all its branches; to voyageurs; and to wives, children, and absent members. The feasting, drinking, and singing bore no comparison with any other event, as Landmann attests. Members included James McGill, founder of McGill University, the principal Nor'Wester agents and their cronies, and all the great wintering partners of yesteryear. Visitors might include John Jacob Astor from New York, spying out the secrets of the northern trade, or various royal travelers, men of the law or candidates under scrutiny for membership. The Beaver was Canada's oldest club, founded in 1785 under the motto "Fortitude in Distress." It became the model for the Canada Club in London, a still surviving dining society that Mackenzie joined as an entitled founding member.

First among equals, Mackenzie ruled among Canadian fur traders. He guarded his hard-won preeminence. He sought to crush any pretender who might seek to subvert the empire in pelts based in Montreal. When a new and surprising challenge to his system of communications into the northwestern interior presented itself, he took immediate steps to cut it off at its source.

One could not imagine a person more different from Mackenzie than his new, unwelcome rival. Thomas Douglas, fifth earl of Selkirk, was a fellow Scot, from the borders of Scotland. He was a liberal-minded, university-educated man with philanthropic leanings. Shy and timid, he took to his pen to advance his schemes. Heir to landed wealth, the high-minded Selkirk had wild dreams of resettling Celtic peoples overseas. He claimed, variously it seems, that organized settlement in Canada could be a cure for recurrent Irish disorders and that the dispossessed people of the Highlands would benefit from assisted emigration to British North America. The schemes he advanced—in Prince Edward Island, Upper Canada, and Red River—were altruistic and to some degree ahead of their times. He read Mackenzie's *Voyages from Montreal* at the time of its publication, and the very next year he advanced his own scheme in London. Acquiring territory on the upper Mississippi as a new home for disadvantaged Scots or Irish became his dream.

Mackenzie scented trouble ahead. Planting a colony at or near the forks of the Red and Assiniboine Rivers, and thus interrupting the local business on which so much of the distant fur trading depended, seemed to Mackenzie a deliberate attempt, backed by the Hudson's Bay Company, to wage war on the North West Company. The staple of the fur traders' diet was pemmican. Pemmican, made from buffalo meat, was based on an open prairie; settlement would introduce a farming economy. He also saw it as a personal vendetta directed against himself. For a time the government took his side. The permanent under-secretary in charge of British policy on such matters, John King, contended that *bloc* or *en masse* settlements—that is, organized settlements under sponsorship of companies and with their own distinct governments—were not practicable, and in any case they would disturb the fur traders. For these reasons Selkirk's Irish project had to be set aside. However, in 1803 Selkirk did succeed in bringing 800 Highlanders to Prince Edward Island.

For a time Selkirk remained satisfied with the state of his imperial schemes for planting settlers in Canada. But marriage into the powerful Wedderburn-Colvile family connection of major investors in the Hudson's Bay Company led him to scheme for control of the Hudson's Bay Company itself. All circumstances seemed in his favor: Europe continued to be convulsed in war; Napoleon's exclusive trade arrangements on the Continent had cut into the fur traffic; Hudson's Bay Company shareholders hardly ever saw a sixpence in dividend. In fact, company shares were going cheap on the London stock exchange. In direct and obvious rivalry to Mackenzie, Selkirk feverishly bought up shares in the Hudson's Bay Company. A race to take over the majority of shares was under way. Mackenzie himself bought as many shares as he could, all of them for the North West Company, he stated. He looked for William McGillivray to do likewise, but McGillivray was absent on one critical occasion, thus allowing some £30,000 worth of Hudson's Bay Company stock to slip into Selkirk's eager hands. Mackenzie alone could not prevent the takeover that Selkirk had engineered, and he resented McGillivray's negligence. He vigorously chided fellow Nor'Westers for not trying to block the arch-rival.

Now Mackenzie's only recourse was to wage a campaign against the contender. In 1808 Mackenzie commenced his attack on Selkirk. "He will put the North West Company to a greater expense," he wrote of Selkirk, "than you seem to apprehend." So he warned his associates. And with a hint that the Nor'Westers had done too little, too late, he added: "had the Company sacrificed £20,000, which might have secured a preponderance in the stock of the Hudson's Bay Company, it would have been money well spent."

By 1810 Selkirk, with the help of relatives, had won ownership by a large margin after nine years of quiet stock accumulation. This allowed him to shape the affairs of the concern to his liking. In the year following, at the general court of the Hudson's Bay Company held in London, the directors gave Earl Selkirk deed to 116,000 square miles of one of the most fertile districts in all of North America. Selkirk called it Assiniboia. Five times the size of Scotland, this wide possession straddled the forty-ninth parallel; though mainly in Manitoba, it included parts of North Dakota and Minnesota. Selkirk had no intention of going there himself, and he called for help from Captain Miles Macdonell for purposes of settling the territory and bringing in a modicum of law and order, in keeping with the British statute of 1803. A strong but unstable Highlander, Macdonell had been a wilderness soldier who had trekked with the Loyalists and Johnson's Mohawks to Canada during the American Revolution. He and Alexander Mackenzie were boy soldiers together in the Mohawk Valley and were probably acquainted with one another. A generation later, in 1812, as governor of Assiniboia, Captain Macdonell led an advance party to set up the Red River Settlement.

In more favorable circumstances, Macdonell could have been an empire builder of renown, but he showed himself to be irascible and undiplomatic. During the next few years Scottish settlers arrived via Hudson Bay. They encountered difficulties at every turn. Destitution and starvation stared them in the face. In addition to the appalling winter cold, crop failures and the blight of the locust in summer lay across the land. Rodents, scurvy, and floods stood in the way of health and safety.

Pemmican was then the lifeblood of the fur trade. This dried and pounded buffalo meat, mixed with grease and flavored with berries, was stored in large ninety-pound bags and shipped as required for provisions for fur trade personnel. Peter Pond, who introduced this commodity in 1779, first brought it from the Chipewyan. North West Company posts along the banks of the Red, Assiniboine, and North Saskatchewan Rivers produced pemmican in large quantities. Storehouses of such an important staple of the fur trade offered tempting targets for Macdonell's lieutenants. On 8 January 1814 Macdonell, as governor of Assiniboia and Selkirk's agent, made a proclamation, known as the Pemmican Proclamation, that forbade the export of pemmican from the colony for a year.

The Métis of Red River, who hunted buffalo and made a business of pemmican production, were the first to suffer, their livelihood placed in serious danger. For a time they had been quiescent and indeed had aided both fur trader and settler in the emerging economy. Highly productive fur traders and superb freighters, they had not yet developed a sense of nationhood—that is, until North West Company agents, such as Duncan Cameron, induced them to defend their own interests. They would respond to Macdonell's fiat in their own fashion and in their own time.

Meanwhile, the Nor'Westers had determined to add to the misery of the settlers and to halt their progress. Mackenzie, now headquartered in London, had always put up a vigorous fight against Selkirk on the home front. When visited by Macdonell at his John Street residence in London in May 1811, Mackenzie denounced the colonial plans of Lord Selkirk as a "mad scheme." Mackenzie knew of the Scottish laird's plans to ruin the fur-trading Nor'Westers. Mackenzie warned Macdonell that the North West Company would cut out the colony and, if necessary, would incite the natives against it.

These were no idle threats, and soon thereafter Mackenzie put in place arrangements designed to halt the flow of emigrants at the source. He placed reports in the newspaper *Inverness Journal* discrediting this "Utopian project" and warning of inhospitable circumstances for any would-be farming emigrants. Copies of this newspaper mysteriously appeared everywhere that Selkirk's emissaries went in search of colonists. Mackenzie employed his own agents and used his own friends. In Stornoway the customs collector, a Mr. Reid, a distant relative of Alexander Mackenzie, subjected the emigrants to every formality and warned them of breaches of contract. Meanwhile a "Captain" Mackenzie, Reid's son-in-law, bribed these same emigrants with the king's shillings to keep them from sailing in Selkirk's three emigrant ships destined for Hudson Bay and then for settlement in Red River. The task of keeping those emigrants aboard the vessels had been a herculean labor in the face of such determined pressures, Macdonell admitted. Even so the ships sailed for Hudson Bay, now some months late for delivering their human cargo to the mouth of the Nelson River and York Factory, from where they would travel to Assiniboia, in time to get settled in for the winter.

Mackenzie had pledged himself to unequivocal, decisive opposition to the colony, using every means in his power. As early as June 1811, before the first of Selkirk's ships left Stornoway for Hudson Bay, Simon McGillivray, partner in the North West Company, wrote to an associate in Montreal of a meeting that he had held with Sir Alexander Mackenzie and Edward Ellice. They had agreed that an express should be sent from Montreal to Red River to warn Nor'Westers to prepare for a year of trial. It was not necessary to detail the particulars of this opposition, McGillivray added, leaving that matter to those on the spot. "It will require some time," he later wrote, "and I fear cause much expense to us as well as to himself [Selkirk], before he is driven to abandon the project; and yet *he must be driven to abandon it,* for his success would strike at the very existence of our Trade."

In the Northwest the fur traders plotted to lay siege to the settlers and to make their lives as miserable as possible. The old struggle between the North West Company and the XY Company, now in the past, had accustomed these men to frontier struggle. It was easy then, in the absence of police or garrisoned troops, to sack and pillage as required. The Nor'Westers, said William McGillivray, had no intention of standing idly by while the opposition plundered and destroyed fur traders' property. The North West Company entered upon a systematic plan to waste Hudson's Bay Company trade. In addition to petty irritations, the Nor'Westers cut down their rivals' stockades, stole fishnets, and frightened trade away. At Isle-à-la-Crosse, for instance, Peter Fidler of the Hudson's Bay Company complained of the terrorist activities of one Samuel Black, who had learned his tricks with the XY Company. "Some people reading this Journal," wrote Fidler in dismay, "might very naturally suppose, that many of the Ill actions that has been done was by people in a state of inebriety—but they are very sober people—it is a systematic plan that has been laid at Grand Portage to harass & distress us."

In the Red River colony, too, the Nor'Westers retaliated. They treated with contempt any and all of Macdonell's proclamations of authority. Such unauthorized edicts as the Pemmican Proclamation infringed on traders' depots and places for collection of provisions for the fur business. Governor Macdonell's belligerence grew, and with it his emotional instability. Fur trade and settlement, long considered to be incompatible in the wilderness, now faced a moment of crisis and of decision.

The Seven Oaks incident took place on 19 June 1816, a few miles from Fort Douglas in the Red River Settlement. The violence of this encounter showed what savage guerilla tactics the Nor'Westers and Métis could employ. The immediate origins of this episode, unique in Canadian history, date from earlier that year, when the Hudson's Bay Company and Selkirk seized and laid waste the Nor'Westers' Fort Gibraltar, strategically located at the forks of the Red and Assiniboine Rivers. By this bold stroke they exposed all fur brigades using the river. And their timing was perfect, for they did so just when pemmican was being carried downriver to meet the fur-trading Nor'westers returning to their rendezvous at Fort William, Lake Superior. By happenstance, farther west, near Seven Oaks at Brandon House, the leader of the Métis, Cuthbert Grant, encountered the Hudson's Bay Company's local governor, Robert Semple, and a dozen of his men. What happened then was not premeditated. Grant had his confederates encircle Semple and his band, and in the ensuing clash Semple and twenty

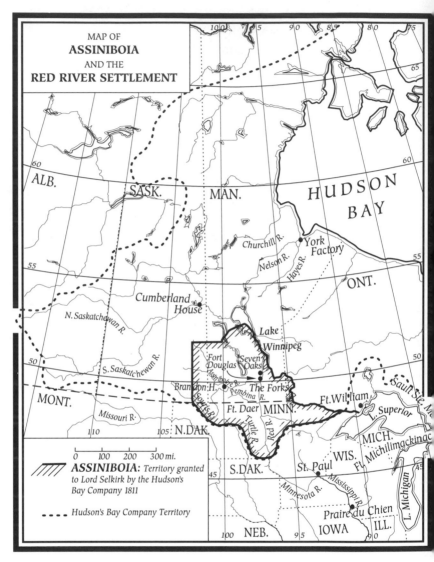

MAP OF
ASSINIBOIA
AND THE
RED RIVER SETTLEMENT

ALB.　SASK.　MAN.　HUDSON BAY

Churchill R.　York Factory

Nelson R.　Hayes R.

ONT.

Cumberland House

N. Saskatchewan R.

Lake Winnipeg

S. Saskatchewan R.

Fort Douglas　Seven Oaks

Assiniboine R.

Brandon H.　The Forks

MONT.　Pembina R.

Ft. Daer　MINN.　Ft. William

Souris R.

Missouri R.　L. Superior

Turtle R.　Red R.

110　105 N.DAK.　MICH.

Sault Ste. M.

Ft. Michilimackinac

0　100　200　300 mi.

WIS.

ASSINIBOIA: *Territory granted
to Lord Selkirk by the Hudson's
Bay Company 1811*

S.DAK.　St. Paul

Minnesota R.　Mississippi R.

L. Michigan

- - - - *Hudson's Bay Company Territory*

Prairie du Chien

NEB.　IOWA　ILL.

6. Assiniboia and the Red River Settlement, showing territory granted
to Lord Selkirk by the Hudson's Bay Company, 1811. This settlement
stood right across the axis of North West Company trade routes and
threatened the pemmican supplies of the fur traders.

of the Hudson's Bay Company's people were killed. Grant's party suffered only one casualty. Selkirk retaliated, capturing Fort William and then reoccupying Fort Douglas. He engaged a mercenary regiment, the De Meurons from Switzerland. He appointed his own agents to arrest leading men of the opposition, including William McGillivray. Mackenzie was safely away from all of this in Britain.

For all intents and purposes the Red River colony had been destroyed: the crops trampled underfoot, the buildings burned, and the settlers sent away. "The colony," wrote Nor'Wester Simon McGillivray, "has been all knocked on the head."

News of these flames of war on the Canadian prairies traveled swiftly to London. For some years the Colonial Office had been distressed at the violence on the Canadian frontier. It now began to agitate for a merger of the two giant concerns involved in the dispute. The colonial secretary, Lord Bathurst, regarded the Selkirk settlement scheme as "wild and unpromising" in any event. Accordingly, he turned his attention to reconciliation. In 1821 he brought about the amalgamation of the North West Company and the Hudson's Bay Company, though enmities did not soon evaporate and suspicion remained the order of the day. Selkirk, suffering from tuberculosis, retired from the business with a cloud over him, facing a variety of litigation and court challenges. He and Mackenzie had settled out of court some years earlier, in 1812, after Mackenzie prepared a bill to charge Selkirk before the lord chancellor in London.

We can only imagine what role Mackenzie played in the sordid horrors at Red River and in the pemmican war. Certainly he is not clear of blame. At an early stage Simon McGillivray had told his brother William in Montreal that Earl Selkirk "is a designing and dangerous character—and Sir Alexander has not been sufficiently aware of him." But

Mackenzie, we know, sought to counter Selkirk's run on Hudson's Bay Company shares, and it seems as if McGillivray, who often was ill-informed in any event, was himself late to realize what was happening. In fact, everyone's hands were bloodied in the Red River affair. "Occurrences with Lord Selkirk and the H B Company are so various," Alexander wrote Roderick on 14 January 1819, "that it would require a volume to detail and comment upon them. . . . Upon the whole they have not turned out so disastrous to the North West Company as might naturally have been apprehended." For awhile fur prices remained high, the profits to the shareholding partners bullish, and the trade buoyant. Thus, when merger came it was the Canadian trade that was the stronger and more powerful, so that the Hudson's Bay Company name was kept for convenience. A revolution had been completed in the charter-holding company, and Montreal and the river empire of the St. Lawrence entered on a rejuvenated phase, another progression in the transcontinental foundations laid down by Champlain and Frontenac, Pond and Mackenzie.

CHAPTER 7

The Legacy and the Canadian Frontier

IN November 1805, just before Mackenzie left Montreal for London, he wrote to his cousin Roderick of his mixed emotions at leaving. "Never mind the folly of the times," he said, "for my own part I am determined to make myself as comfortable as circumstances will allow. I have a large field before me. I do not leave Canada without regret." Indeed, much "folly of the times" then existed. A state of war continued for the British, and merchant shipping could always be intercepted by privateers or else by French or Spanish warships. The American government fumed at Britain's high-handed actions against U.S. citizens serving as British merchant sailors. For his part, however, Mackenzie sailed in relative security. He had luckily been able to take passage in the handsome thirty-two-gun British frigate HMS *Pallas,* commanded by Thomas Lord Cochrane, Earl of Dundonald, the eye-catching, stock-jobbing, controversial independence fighter of later years. In leaving the Canadian port Mackenzie anticipated a pleasant passage. He no doubt enjoyed the bounty of the captain's dining table. Certainly this was a crossing quite different in character from his westward passage as a mere emigrant three decades before.

In following months Mackenzie enjoyed his old London haunts and also traveled to Scotland. News reaching him from Roderick in Canada continued to report good earnings from the *pays d'en haut;* very handsome profits were yielded on all outgoing expenses. North West Company fortunes continued to rise. As an author, too, Mackenzie enjoyed similarly promising signs. His book was enjoying excellent sales, with editions in French and German in print. There was even talk of a new edition of his voyages. "I had not the most distant idea that it was the intention of the Company to give the History of the North West," he wrote Roderick, obviously believing that Nor'West partners intended to infringe on his literary genius. "[A]nd now instead of asking your assistance," he said in reference to Roderick's help to him of yesteryear, "I offer you mine as you are the person that seems to take the lead."

In the end, regrettably, no independent history of the fur trade came from Roderick's pen. But at that time, when Roderick had the project under consideration, Alexander counseled him to tell all the truth about their contemporaries. He warned Roderick of the difficulties he would have to face before the book could be finished. "Your object must be to relate matters as they occurred which may make more enemies than friends," he advised. "Besides you will have to advance at least two thousand pounds before you receive a shilling for the work." Perhaps Alexander Mackenzie had paid to get his own book into print? Others sometimes got advances from publishers. Mackenzie was particularly interested in Samuel Hearne's travels and advised his cousin to ask the English Chief and any Chipewyan for the fullest account they could provide of Hearne's journey to the north ocean. The public wondered if Hearne had reached the mouth of the Coppermine River and had seen the Arctic Ocean. Mackenzie wanted this matter put to rest.

In his latter years in London and in Scotland, Alexander Mackenzie took steps to enrich his business connections in the fur trade. His earnings grew by leaps and bounds. In 1808 in cash assets alone he had in Canada about £27,000; in the four years beginning in 1808 he acquired £5323 in Hudson's Bay Company stocks, a fortune in those days. His legal papers, particularly his litigations against Selkirk, fill volumes in the Hudson's Bay Company archives and await serious study. After his death, his Hudson's Bay Company shares were sold in block lots. The fur trade had given Mackenzie his wealth, and in Britain he was able to complete the cycle of wealth creation. He did not come home, as many Scots did, paradoxically, wealthy from overseas enterprises but impoverished by schemes taken up at home. Rather the reverse was true, for this sojourner in Canada, made rich by trade and famous by corporate wars as well as by writing, took up his last challenges—in British finance and trade.

In 1812, at the age of fifty, Sir Alexander Mackenzie married Geddes Margaret Mackenzie, a remarkably young beauty, age fourteen. They were of the same clan but not related directly by bloodline. Geddes Margaret Mackenzie descended from the second earl of Seaforth; her paternal grandparents were Captain John Mackenzie and Geddes Mackenzie.

Captain John Mackenzie had acquired the handsome estate of Avoch in the Black Isle, Ross and Cromarty. Sitting rather high on a rising headland, overlooking forests, fields, and the magnificent Moray Firth, Avoch House was a seat fit for a king, especially one with an eye to agricultural improvements, fishing, and shipping. The heir to Avoch and its estates was George Mackenzie, Geddes Margaret's father, and upon his death Geddes and her twin sister, Margaret Elizabeth, came into possession of it by their father's will. In 1812, the same year as his marriage, Sir Alexander Mackenzie, "now or late of John Street, American Square, London," purchased the estates of Avoch. Thus did Geddes Mackenzie's ancestral seat stay in her control, through the purchasing arrangements of her husband.

The married couple spent summers at Avoch and undertook modernizations and improvements to the house, buildings, and grounds. The village that lies below the house was then a fishing village. When local improvements were advantageous, Sir Alexander ordered a stone wall and wharves to be built there, as well as a seawall between Avoch and Fortrose, where there was a good school. A road leading northeast from the Mackenzie manor house, behind the church where he was later buried, brought the walker to a cluster of well-built stone houses and a school for young children. Down in the town a woollen mill was started. Mackenzie arranged for the planting of an oysterbed in the Bay of Munlochy. From time to time the barque *Sir Alexander Mackenzie*, which plied the waters to and from Stornoway, could be seen in the offing. Present-day informants advise that Sir Alexander and Lady Mackenzie undertook various improvements in the town and on the estates.

In baronial splendor, representative of the Scotland of that age, Alexander and Geddes Mackenzie lived out pleasant and productive days. When not in Avoch the Mackenzies resided in London with family and friends. They lived in Jermyn Street for a time and then removed to Clarges Street in still more fashionable Piccadilly, a property kept for many years after Sir Alexander's death. Here Highland balls were held for many years. Like many another wealthy London Scots family, they led an active social life.

From the union of Sir Alexander and Lady Mackenzie were born three children: a daughter, Margaret Geddes, in 1816; a son, Alexander George, in 1818; and a second son, George, in 1819. This new generation of Mackenzies had half-brothers and half-sisters in Canada and its Northwest Territories whom they would never know. One of Sir Alexander Mackenzie's Métis sons, perhaps a child of his native wife The Catt, was named Andrew. A fur trader himself, he died at Fort Vermilion on 1 March 1809 in the general starvation that faced many in the Athabasca country, a starvation brought about by the fur-trading wars and by the desperately cold conditions of forested northern lands in winter. Sir Alexander Mackenzie continued to provide for his native family. In Mackenzie's letters to trusty Roderick there are references to a Mrs. Mackenzie of Trois Rivières and to a Kitty who needs caring for; one can only surmise that Kitty is The Catt, who died at Fort Chipewyan about ten years after Mackenzie had left Athabasca. Or Kitty may have been their daughter.

Among Sir Alexander Mackenzie's many letters to Roderick, the last is the most poignant, certainly the most plaintive. Mackenzie, now in his mid-fifties, was feeling the effects of the years. Twenty-six years earlier, while he forded the streams of the Peace and trudged the pathways of the western plateau, the wear and tear on the body, the herculean exertions of this explorer, had begun to take their toll. Leaving aside the mental strains and sheer exhaustion of such hazardous feats, the physical efforts often in the face of starvation must have been phenomenal. Mackenzie was a hard-drinking, hard-driving man. The signs of decay were there. His ankles were so swollen and so painful in the summer of 1793 that he had to be carried in places. These, Dr. Mark Wade speculated, were the early symptoms of chronic nephritis, called after 1827 Bright's Disease, a debilitating and ultimately fatal disorder relating to various forms of bacterial infection and involving the gradual degeneration and shrinkage of the kidneys. In Mackenzie's time the medical profession had little understanding of kidney failure. The description of his symptoms, given in his letter to Roderick, suggests to Dr. John Naish some form of chronic anemia with consequent anoxia of the brain on exercise or, just possibly, chronic heart failure. Diet and rest could prolong life, but not for long.

Thus Mackenzie penned that last, sweet letter to Roderick, dated Avoch, 14 January 1819:

I have been overtaken with the consequences of my sufferings in the North West. . . . [I]t has not as yet arrived at a severe crisis. I have in obedience to orders become a water drinker and milk sop. I have not tasted wine, spirituous or malt liquor for several months, which I think has been of service to me. The symptoms of the disorder are very disagreeable and most uncomfortable. The exercise of walking, particularly if uphill, brings on a headache, stupor of dead pain, which at once pervades the whole frame, attended with a listlessness and apathy which I cannot well describe. Exercise in a carriage, if not violent, has a beneficial effect. The great Doctor Hamilton of Edinburgh calls it a shake of the constitution and I am acting now under his guidance.

Mackenzie was a year away from death and, ever thinking forward, encouraged Roderick to send his son to Thain or Fortrose in Scotland for his education. "I shall have a little fellow, if God spare him, this day eleven months old that would accompany him. Our little girl is very thriving. Her mother has not recovered her usual health since her last confinement." He closed his last letter: "Lady Mackenzie is sitting by me and the children are playing on the floor. The former joins me most cordially in kind regards to you Mrs McKenzie and your young family." Thus ended a remarkable correspondence and friendship, not without its difficulties at mid-passage, but true to the last.

In January 1820, while his hated rival Selkirk was fighting against terminal tuberculosis in the Pyrenees, Sir Alexander Mackenzie traveled with his wife and children by coach to Edinburgh to see his physician. He died on the return journey to Avoch. He was suddenly taken ill at Mulinearn, near Dunkeld, on 11 March and died the following morning. His body was taken to Avoch, where he was buried on 20 March. Lady Mackenzie built a memorial enclosure in the churchyard, where plaques and tablets now recount the vital details of the explorer's life and those of his kin. Legal wrangles followed, and it was not until 1830, after threatening to take the Hudson's Bay Company to court, that Lady Mackenzie finally succeeded in obtaining an out-of-court settlement for £30,000 owed to her from her husband's interest in Sir Alexander Mackenzie & Company.

Mackenzie's phenomenal travels continue to inspire those who study the history of northern and wilderness travel. In addition, they print indelibly in our memory the difficulties of long-range commerce. By joining transcontinental trade with Pacific coast maritime commerce, Mackenzie stood at the front lines of commerce. He had not discovered a navigable waterway, as he readily admitted. His mind jumped ahead of terrestrial obstacles, and he realized that if lines of communication and a network of trading bases could be established, the fur trade could encompass the great bounty of seaborne commerce. If developed with British capital and expertise, a new commerce between Europe and Asia could be undertaken. "By opening this intercourse between the Atlantic and Pacific Oceans," he urged in his *Voyages*, "and forming regular establishments through the interior, at both extremes, as well as along the coasts and islands, the entire command of the fur trade of North America might be obtained. . . . To this might be added the fishing in both seas and the markets of the four quarters of the globe."

In that age, as the secretary of the Board of Trade, Henry Dundas, observed, the spirit of commercial adventure among the British was unbounded. A few years after Mackenzie's achievements, British statesmen were admitting that the trade to China held the greatest prospect for future growth. By 1821 the Nor'Westers had erected an organization that was transcontinental in scope, leading Canadian historian Harold Innis to observe in the 1920s that the North West Company was the forerunner of Canadian confederation and that the foundations of the dominion of Canada had been securely laid. Canadian trade to Asia, though in its infancy, stood on the threshold of mighty profit. Two centuries after Mackenzie's arrival, the port of Vancouver shipped more tonnage than all the east coast Canadian ports together. If the fur trade was the precursor of modern Canada, then Mackenzie stands as one of the chief national architects, for exploration preceded settlement, railways, and treaties with the native peoples. Such a claim may exceed historical reality; Mackenzie never imagined himself as a nation builder. Commercial expansion, and its relationship to imperial power, was altogether different in his mind. Even so, Mackenzie stands at the leading edge of an ever expanding system of empire based in Montreal, New York, London, and elsewhere.

The learned Scottish political economist Adam Smith remarked in his *Wealth of Nations,* published in 1776, that the discovery of America and the passage to eastern seas constituted the most important events recorded in the history of mankind. Taking this claim at face value, we can conclude that Mackenzie's journeys and their findings brought together these two historic vectors of human enterprise and achievement. The discovery of North America was largely completed because of Mackenzie's journeys north and west. Moreover, he showed that although there was no water passage, trade could still be undertaken to China and Japan. One thing was certain: the great sea of the West did not exist, and no westward navigable stream was to be found. Other explorers—Simon Fraser, David Thompson, and Samuel Black—filled in the yawning gaps in Mackenzie's great 1801 map. When Aaron Arrowsmith, court cartographer in London, issued various new editions of his grand sheet showing the shores, waters, and other geographical features of northern North America, Mackenzie's discoveries were the benchmark from which all new additional scraps of information had to be measured.

Even so, for a brief time a shadow of doubt was cast on Mackenzie's findings. Truth does not easily displace misguided speculation. Captain George Vancouver's survey of the northwest coast had killed any idea of a Pacific entrance to a northwest passage in southerly latitudes, that is, south of northern Alaska and the Bering Sea. But already Scottish students of geography had proclaimed the scientific discoveries of their fur-trading countrymen. In 1805 David Macpherson, who would nowadays be classified as an astute global business analyst, studied the voyage and travel literature of the age. In commenting on the events of 1793, the same year when Vancouver and Mackenzie almost bumped into one another near Dean Channel on the Pacific, Macpherson wrote bluntly that Mackenzie's "journey, or voyage of discovery, and also that of Mr. Hearne in the year 1771, having stretched across all the unfrequented regions of America, ought surely to be sufficient to prove the utter impossibility of the existence of a navigable communication in any temperate part of that continent." He added that he hoped that "we might reasonably expect to have no more conjectures or speculations on that subject."

Mackenzie used all information that came to him to good effect. From that crabbed genius Pond he borrowed all the necessary information to find the great western river and full particulars as to how to enlarge the trade of Athabasca. Pond's ideas were neither as extravagant nor as foolish as they were portrayed at the time. Though wrong as to details, they were correct in concept. Only on-the-ground evaluation could end speculation as to the course of such a river. Mackenzie failed, or neglected, to give credit where credit was due to Pond for pioneering achievement and geographic trade strategy. Mackenzie exhibited the triumph of the human will in his two great voyages of discovery. His ego and desire for attention compelled him to scrub the past of his debt to Peter Pond, who deserves a better fate than neglect and maligning.

Mackenzie went on his expedition in hopes of getting into Cook's River, or Cook Inlet. To establish "the practicability of penetrating across the continent" was truly "the favourite project of my ambition." Although disappointed in this, he proved beyond doubt that no northwest passage existed below this latitude. He erred, however, when he speculated in his Journal: "I believe it will be generally allowed that no passage is practicable in higher latitude, the Sea being eternally covered with Ice." Nowadays submarines and icebreakers make the passage. However, the Arctic coasting journeys of Franklin and of Beechey demonstrated that even if boats were not crushed on rock or ice, then exploring parties might sometimes fall prey to hostile natives. The immense, unforgiving frozen sea that Mackenzie, Franklin, Beechey, and others uncomfortably fixed their eyes upon offered a physical barrier of limitless magnitude in an era before technological triumphs, particularly icebreakers and aircraft, revolutionized Arctic transportation. Mackenzie spoke for his time.

Mackenzie's discoveries helped shape the discourse on geographical inquiry and polar science of Regency Britain. When the young assistant secretary of the Admiralty, John Barrow, in the tradition of Sir Joseph Banks, set forth the outlines for a program of Arctic exploration, Mackenzie's discovery of the polar sea at the mouth of the river that bears his name constituted one of four points that indicated the northernmost shore of the American continent and the margins of a northwest passage. Taken together with Hearne's verification of an Arctic sea at the mouth of the Coppermine, Mackenzie's river estuary at saltwater formed the central location of a quartet of points linking an eastern entry to a passage to the Pacific with Cook's Icy Cape, Alaska. In an era when the British government had posted rewards of £20,000 for discovering a northwest passage and £5,000 for reaching the North Pole, the verification of the mouths of the Mackenzie and Coppermine Rivers contributed to the ending of geographical speculation in respect to two specific locations. The search for the northwest passage did not die with Mackenzie and was deflected north to higher latitudes. The concept was reshaped by Barrow at the Admiralty, aided and abetted by the likes of Captains Franklin, Ross, Parry, and Beechey. In its new and convenient guise the quest consumed the attention of the interested public for much of the nineteenth century and even later. New objectives were added to the pursuit: the penetration of icy barriers, the testing of ice flow patterns, the investigation of ice breakups. The commercial pursuits of Alexander Mackenzie had given way to an altogether different set of goals. All sorts of expeditions were mounted, on the necessary and irrefutable grounds of advancement of science, pursuit of commerce, maintenance of national sovereign interests, protection against foreign encroachment, and even the useful employment of otherwise idle naval officers, men, and ships. In stark contrast to these elaborate schemes, Mackenzie's self-directed, one-hundred-day voyage by bark canoe to the polar sea stands as a testament—as did Amundsen's South Pole triumph, to say nothing of his northwest passage sweep—to the advantages of small expeditions.

On 7 November 1805 Lewis and Clark came near the great ocean that they had been so long anxious to see. During the next week they reconnoitered the immense estuary of the river of the West so long talked of by Carver, Mackenzie, and other visionaries. By their passage overland, astonishing enough in its difficulty, they had done what government had ordered. Twelve years before, Mackenzie had stolen the prize of being the first European to cross the continent. A cranky publisher, who thought the American discoverers were receiving too much merit for too little achievement too lately accomplished, denigrated Meriwether Lewis's

achievements. Lewis had been honored with the governor-
ship of Upper Louisiana, and on 7 April 1807 the critic wrote
acidly to Governor Lewis:

> With respect to the hazardous nature of the enterprise and the
> courage necessary for undertaking it, candour compels me to
> say, that public opinion has placed them on too high ground.
> Mr. M'Kenzie with a party consisting of about one fourth part
> of the number under your command, with means which will
> not bear a comparison with those furnished you, and without
> the *authority*, the *flags*, or *medals* of government, crossed the
> Rocky mountains several degrees north of your route, and for
> the *first time* penetrated to the Pacific Ocean. You had the
> advantage of the information contained in his journal, and
> could in some degree estimate and guard against the dangers
> and difficulties you were to meet; . . . had government given
> an invitation, hundreds as daring, enterprising and capable of
> your Excellency, would have offered to engage in the expedi-
> tion, and for compensations much smaller that were received
> by yourself and other persons composing the corps actually
> engaged in it.

Mackenzie is best evaluated in the Canadian and British
imperial context. To a large degree this private trader, rival
of the great companies of the day, had robbed the official
circles of British government and geographical science of
one of its greatest, most sought-after prizes. His dual thrusts
into the wilderness, unauthorized save by himself and denigrated by fellow partners in the North West Company,
brought geographical results that ships of the Royal Navy,
schemes of Sir Joseph Banks, or mental machinations and
writings of Alexander Dalrymple could not achieve even at
great expense to taxpayers. In other words, Mackenzie
stands outside of the pack of internal fixers who dominated
late eighteenth-century British geographical science. His
victory is all the sweeter because he did it on his own.
Dalrymple and Banks might dismiss the likes of Peter Pond

as unscientific and even counter to the interests of the British Empire. The empire could strike back against Pond. It could not do so against Mackenzie. In the end Mackenzie defied them all, and to this day his life exemplifies determination, endurance, and dedication to a task that he and he alone first achieved.

Pathfinder of Canada's empire both north and west, Mackenzie spanned the land from sea to sea. By canoe and portage he sought the northwest passage and the fabled link to Russia, Japan, and China. He found something far greater: the wealth of a slumbering half-continent. Giant among a special breed of fur traders known as Nor'Westers, he opened Canada to its western destiny. His achievements, in exploration as in commerce, rested on European capital and markets, on native trading and advice, and on French Canadian grit and brawn. But he alone drove on the expeditions to their goals. In yet another way he showed that labor could be the basis of wealth. His life demonstrated Adam Smith's maxim that every individual could improve his fortune and thereby rise in the world on the basis of his own labor. For Mackenzie the fur trade offered just such a means to the accumulation of wealth. The benefits of commerce were his to gain and keep. Yet he saw them also as means for the useful production of wealth beneficial to the prosperity of the British Empire.

APPENDIX I

Mackenzie Place-Names

MACKENZIE and his expeditions left a trail of place-names. Alan Rayburn in *Canadian Geographic* ([June–July 1989]: 84–85) provides particulars and explanations of these place-names. Franklin named a point near the mouth of the Coppermine River for Mackenzie; it is now *Mackenzie Point*. *Mackenzie Bay* lies at the mouth of the *Mackenzie Delta* of the *Mackenzie River;* these are all official designations, as are the following. The *District of Mackenzie* is one of three divisions of the Northwest Territories. The system of mountains and ranges from the Liard to the Ramparts River and west to the Yukon border is called the *Mackenzie Mountains*. The *Mackenzie Highway* links Grimshaw, Alberta, with Hay River, NWT, and goes north to Fort Simpson and Wrigley.

In British Columbia is found the *District Municipality of Mackenzie*. Across the *Mackenzie Valley* and over *Mackenzie Pass,* one has a view of *Mount Mackenzie*. There is, besides, a *Mount Sir Alexander* north of McBride and a *Fort Alexandria* on the Fraser, both named for the explorer. *Mackenzie Rock,* near Bella Coola, is contained in *Sir Alexander Mackenzie Provincial Park*. "With 11 features named for Sir Alexander Mackenzie in the Northwest Territories and British Columbia, including Canada's longest river," writes Rayburn, "it may be well argued that Mackenzie has been adequately honored. But other than in schools in Edmonton and Inuvik, the explorer does not appear to have been remembered in the names of the nation's institutions—an oversight that perhaps one day will be corrected."

APPENDIX 2

Mackenzie's Advice to Lt. John Franklin, R.N., 1819

This material is drawn from Scott Polar Research Institute, Cambridge, England, SPRI MS 248/276, pp. 29–31, and is reprinted by permission.

London 21st May 1819

Dear Sir,

Being convinced you will by the letter [in Public Record Office, London, C.O. 6/15, fols. 99–101] of Mr [Simon] McGillivary to the Gentlemen of the North West Company residing in that Country receive every aid & supply which they can possibly afford to further and promote the object of your expedition, it is only necessary for me to suggest my Ideas of the Plan which I think you ought to pursue.

Upon your arrival at Your Factory you should not lose an hour of time to prepare and to pursue your journey for which purpose I think two of their largest Canoes will be necessary properly manned and equipped in everything necessary to promote safety and expedition. Amongst the Crew there should be two of the HB Company's old Servants Natives if possible of the Orkneys who have been in the Habits of living in Communication with the Esquimaux and if of this Nation you could procure a Young Man who would be willing to accompany you it might prove an object of great Importance as he could interpret for you on the Sea

Coast [and] Copper Mine River; indeed then these People should be considered as becoming of your Party throughout and tempted by some remuneration in the event of success. Independent of your own Baggage & stores with the Quantity of Provision necessary for your Voyage you should have to embark in these Canoes pieces of Goods for Trade and Barter, Fishing tackling &c for fear you should by the Season or Accident be prevented arriving at the regular Establishments of either Company on your Route to Athabasca and should contain 5 Indian Guns, 1 Keg Powder, 1 Keg Balls, 2 Bag of Shot, 1 case with Iron work assorted 1 Roll of Twist Tobacco, two or three Bales of Dry Goods suitable to the Trade, and if you could provide yourself with shirts & some other Articles that are given to Men as Equipments it would be necessary as they are Articles which used to be scarce and not to be had in the Interior of the Country at the Season you may require them to give to the People that have to accompany you from Athabasca. I should have added to the above Articles a quantity of spirits. Thus prepared it's possible with all the dispatch you can make you may not be able to get further than Isle a la Crosse. In that Event I would recommend that yourself & two or three of your Party with proper Guides should proceed as soon as the ice would permit on foot to Athabasca to make your arrangements for the ensuing spring. By the time you would be ready or the season allowed of your taking your departure your party with proper exertion would join you at Athabasca—being again together a different mode of conveyance will be necessary which of course you will have provided namely one North West Canoe capable of carrying two Tons and Six Indian Canoes. The Complement of People which you will require will hardly be Sufficient to Navigate these Canoes, however you must proceed more slowly, and you will be able to manage as you go with the Current until you come to the Slave Lake. Your Establishment now cannot

APPENDIX 2   215

be less & should not be more than yourselves 6—The two
Orkneymen & the Esquimaux 3—A Clerk 1 Two Steers-
men & Two Foremen 4 Two Indians & their Wives 4 in
all eighteen persons with your Baggage & stores. You will
have to Embark in these Canoes so much Pemacan as they
can carry, with about 10 parcels or Packages of Goods properly assorted for presents & Barter. Should you thus
Equipped be able to reach the Slave Lake before the Ice in
that Lake is broke up I would recommend your leaving your
large Canoe and proceed across the Lake with your small
Canoes and all your Baggage, should it require to make this
transport at two trips, to the entrance of some of these
Rivers falling in from the North and communicating with
a Chain of Small Lakes which I understand lay in a North
direction towards the Copper Mine River—and is the common Route which the Indians take in going to the Country.
Should you apprehend being interrupted in the Slave Lake
by Ice, the Men & Indians should provide wood to make
the Sledges going down the Slave River. Contemplating this
kind of Carriage and Travelling—you sometimes carrying
the Canoes & the Canoes you—you might in course of the
Season after your arrival at Athabasca have an opportunity
of making an appointment with some of the Indians to meet
you on the North Side of the Slave Lake to assist you in
getting forward. The only danger there would be in this is
that they might not provide themselves in provision and
would expect Support from you which would never do.

In selecting your guide I wish you could fall in with my
old Friend if alive Nestabeck commonly called the English
Cheif [sic], he would be invaluable as he was as I told you
often in that Country. Presuming you have surmounted all
your difficulties and reached the Sea at the discharge of the
Copper Mine River—it will I think be absolutely necessary
to find some of the Natives, say the Esquimaux, make your
Peace with them & persuade some of them to accompany

you along the Coast until they give you over to some of their Friends to the East. One of their Large Canoes, or their Womens Canoes, will carry your whole Party, and if they consent to allow some of their Wives and Children to embark it will secure the Men to you who of course will accompany you in their own small Canoe which fair all weather. Should you get to the Sea and could Establish this understanding with the Esquimaux I have no doubt of its being possible to succeed in that object of your ambition, as I am persuaded that the Nation are the same People, and have communication together along the Sea Coast from Hudson's Bay to Behrings Straits which may be and I suppose is interrupted by Ice at different Periods of the year.

If you can glean any thing from this that can assist you in the prosecution of your arduous undertaking it will be gratifying my anxious wish, as I feel earnestly interested in the results of your exertion under such perilous circumstances and believe me

Yours Most Sincerely
Alex Mackenzie

Sources

The following commentary provides a complete guide to the materials, both primary and secondary, used in the writing of this book. Because this is an interpretive reappraisal of Mackenzie rather than a comprehensive or full biography, such documentation as is given here should suffice for the purposes of follow-up research. The commentary is intended as a guide for persons wishing to seek confirmation of the statements found in the text of this book or wishing to learn more about the subject.

Wherever possible, this biography of Alexander Mackenzie rests on his own monumental text of his great travels, *Voyages from Montreal, on the River St. Laurence, Through the Continent of North America, to the Frozen and Pacific Oceans; in the Years 1789 and 1793. With a Preliminary Account of the Rise, Progress and Present State of the Fur Trade of that Country* (London, 1801; reprinted, with an introduction by Roy Daniells, Edmonton: Hurtig, 1971). That masterpiece of exploration literature has enjoyed a phenomenal publication history, and the book remains of the greatest importance in transcontinental and global travel literature. The original work was published in American editions, in New York and Philadelphia. A French translation was published in Paris in 1802, and a German edition appeared in Hamburg in the same year. A two-volume English edition, printed in Edinburgh in 1802, contains—drawn from the French edition—translations of original notes by Bougainville and Volney, both members of the French Senate; these notes add particulars of French posts and trade history, and provide additional details of the trading link from Lake Ontario to Manhattan by the Mohawk and Albany Rivers. Numerous abridged and summary editions of this classic have been printed, including one in Russian (published in St. Petersburg in 1808). A pirated edition of the 1801 edition was published as *Mr. Maclauries' Narrative or Journal of Voyages and Travels Through the North-West*

Continent of America in the Years 1789 and 1789 (London, 1802); a critique of this worthless and inaccurate production may be found in F. W. Howay, "Maclauries' Travels through America," *Washington Historical Quarterly* 23 (1932): 83–87.

In recent times two important partial texts of the *Voyages from Montreal* have been published. These are *Exploring the Northwest Territory: Sir Alexander Mackenzie's Journal of a Voyage by Bark Canoe from Lake Athabasca to the Pacific [sic] Ocean in the Summer of 1789*, edited by T. H. McDonald (Norman: University of Oklahoma Press, 1966), and *First Man West: Alexander Mackenzie's Journal of His Voyage to the Pacific Coast of Canada in 1793*, edited by Walter Sheppe (Berkeley: University of California Press, 1962; reprinted as *Journal of a Voyage to the Pacific* [New York: Dover, 1995]). Between them, the editors of these two volumes traveled much of Mackenzie's routes, and for that reason their notations and historical introductions are of great value. The McDonald book contains a transcription of the only remaining manuscript that served as the basis for the published *Voyages from Montreal;* the original is to be found in the Stowe Collection, Department of Manuscripts, British Library, London.

Special mention must be made of the scholarly edition of Mackenzie's *Voyages* published under the title *The Journals and Letters of Sir Alexander Mackenzie*, edited by W. Kaye Lamb (London: Cambridge University Press for the Hakluyt Society, Extra Series No. 41, 1970). This work includes the maps from the original edition; a portion of Peter Pond's map of northwestern America as prepared for presentation to the empress of Russia, July 1787; maps showing Mackenzie's route to the Arctic and Pacific Oceans on modern maps; and Mackenzie's extant letters for the years 1786–1819. In addition, it is heavily annotated with verifications and variations of place names and site identifications, and contains a brief introduction to the subject and a useful bibliography. This important work also contains the invaluable "General History of the Fur Trade," attributed to Mackenzie's cousin Roderick Mackenzie, with Lamb's valuable annotations.

Biographies of Alexander Mackenzie continue to appear. The following are the principal ones of note: R. M. Ballantyne, *The Pioneers: A Tale of the Western Wilderness Illustrative of the Adventures and Discoveries of Sir Alexander Mackenzie* (London: James Nisbet, 1872), which contains some insights the author garnered from family members; George Bryce, *Mackenzie, Selkirk, Simpson* (Toronto: Morang, 1905), which likewise benefits from family data; Mark S. Wade, *Mackenzie of Canada: The Life and Adventures of Alexander Mackenzie, Discoverer*

(Edinburgh: Blackwood, 1927), the first full-scale treatment of the subject and regarded by many scholars as a classic reference; Hume Wrong, *Sir Alexander Mackenzie, Explorer and Fur-Trader* (Toronto: Macmillan, 1927), aimed principally at a juvenile market; and Arthur Woollacott, *Mackenzie and His Voyageurs: By Canoe to the Arctic and the Pacific, 1789–93* (London: J. M. Dent, 1927); the finely sensitive interpretation by Roy Daniells, *Alexander Mackenzie and the North West* (London: Faber and Faber, 1969); and James K. Smith, *Alexander Mackenzie, Explorer: The Hero Who Failed* (Toronto: McGraw-Hill Ryerson, 1973). See also, W. Kaye Lamb, "Sir Alexander Mackenzie," in *Dictionary of Canadian Biography* (1983   ), 5:537–43. Factually unreliable is Philip Vail (pseudonym of Noel B. Gerson), *The Magnificent Adventures of Alexander Mackenzie* (New York: Dodd, Mead, 1964). As a subject for juvenile literature, Mackenzie has attracted considerable attention, first by R. M. Ballantyne (see above) and in recent years by Ainslie Manson, *Alexander Mackenzie* (Toronto: Grolier, 1988), and Georgia Xydes, *Alexander Mackenzie and the Explorers of Canada* (New York: Chelsea, 1992). Still younger readers will be drawn to Ainslie Manson's *And a Dog Came, Too* (Vancouver: Groundwood, 1992). Mackenzie, like many a Highlander, was bilingual, if not multilingual. He would have spoken Gaelic as a native tongue; it is thus of interest to record that the first known biography of him in that language has appeared: *Alasdair MacChoinnich ann an Canada*, by Fionnlagh MacLeoid (Stornoway: Acair, 1991).

On the editing of the text of Mackenzie's *Voyage from Montreal* and its preparation for publication in 1801, consult Franz Montgomery, "Alexander Mackenzie's Literary Assistant," *Canadian Historical Review* 18 (1937): 301–4. For appraisal of Mackenzie's relevance to recent Canadian history and letters, the following works are useful: Roy Daniells, "The Literary Relevance of Alexander Mackenzie," *Canadian Literature* 38 (Autumn 1968): 19–28; and I. S. MacLaren, "Alexander Mackenzie and the Landscapes of Commerce," *Studies in Canadian Literature* 7 (1982): 141–50.

Special studies of aspects of Mackenzie's life include the following: F. W. Howay, "An Identification of Sir Alexander Mackenzie's Fort Fork," *Transactions of the Royal Society of Canada* 3rd ser., 2 (1928): 165–74; R. P. Bishop, *Mackenzie's Rock, with a Map Showing the Course Followed by the Explorer . . .* (Ottawa: Government Printer, 1925); and Michael Bliss, "Conducted Tour," *Beaver* 69,2 (April–May 1989): 16–24.

No comprehensive, published collection of documents relating to the

North West Company and its various contributing partnerships exists. However, for the study of Alexander Mackenzie's life and times in relation to the North West Company, the following books are useful: L. R. Masson, comp., *Les Bourgeois de la Compagnie du Nord-Ouest*, 2 vols. (Quebec City, 1889–90; reprint, New York: Antiquarian Press, 1960), which contains the "Reminiscences" of Roderick Mackenzie; *Report of the Archives of Canada for the Years 1889 and 1890* (Ottawa: Queen's Printer, 1891), which contains documents on Peter Pond, George Dixon, Isaac and David Ogden, and Alexander Dalrymple concerning the North West Company and British interest in the northwest passage and scientific inquiry in the late eighteenth century; and W. S. Wallace, ed., *Documents Relating to the North West Company* (Toronto: Champlain Society, 1934), which prints surviving corporate agreements as forged by the partners and agents.

North West Company letterbooks, correspondence, and other documents, including maps, are to be found in the National Archives of Canada, Ottawa, and also may be located in certain documentation series of the Hudson's Bay Company Archives in the Archives of the Province of Manitoba (microfilm copies of which are held in the Public Record Office, London, and the National Archives of Canada, Ottawa). In addition, the Haldimand Papers in the British Library, London, contain valued insights into the trade of the Old Northwest in Mackenzie's time, including reports by Captain Brehm and details of explorations. The McCord Museum, McGill University, Montreal, contains many documents relating to the fur trade, at least one Beaver Club medal, and Mrs. Munro's advice to her husband, quoted in the text, on how to become baron of the South Sea. The North West Company needs a new historian, but the profiles of the past are laid down in Gordon C. Davidson, *The North West Company* (1918; reprint, New York: Russell & Russell, 1967), and Marjorie Wilkins Campbell, *The North West Company* (Toronto: Macmillan of Canada, 1957). Concerning the history of the XY Company, special mention should be made of R. Harvey Fleming, "The Origin of Sir Alexander Mackenzie and Company," *Canadian Historical Review* 9, 2 (1928): 137–55; see also Elaine Allan Mitchell, "New Evidence on the Mackenzie-McTavish Break," *Canadian Historical Review* 41 (1960): 41–47.

Journals or narratives of other fur traders of the time are numerous, and some have been published. The following works are cited in the text: Charles Gates, ed., *Five Fur Traders of the Northwest, Being the Narrative of Peter Pond and the Diaries of John Macdonell, Archibald N. McLeod, Hugh Faries, and Thomas Connor* (St. Paul: Minnesota

Historical Society, 1965); Alexander Henry, *Travels and Adventures in Canada and the Indian Territories between the Years 1760 and 1776* (New York, 1809; new edition, edited by James Bain, Toronto, 1901; reprint, New York: Burt Franklin, 1969); W. Kaye Lamb, *Simon Fraser: Letters and Journals* (Toronto: Macmillan of Canada, 1966); Richard Glover, ed., *David Thompson's Narrative* (Toronto: Champlain Society, 1962); and A. S. Morton, ed., *Journal of Duncan M'Gillivray* (Toronto: Macmillan of Canada, 1929). Various volumes of the Hudson's Bay Record Society provide details on this period of North American fur trade history or on aspects of subsequent exploration and trade in the wake of Mackenzie's voyages. See, for instance, *Black's Rocky Mountain Journal, 1824* (London: Hudson's Bay Record Society, 1955). By and large, Hudson's Bay Company archives are silent on Mackenzie's activities.

General surveys of the fur trade and of northern exploration include the following: Harold A. Innis, *The Fur Trade in Canada: An Introduction to Canadian Economic History* (Toronto, 1930; revised edition, with introduction by Robin W. Winks, New Haven: Yale University Press, 1962); E. E. Rich, *The Fur Trade and the Northwest to 1857* (Toronto: McClelland and Stewart, 1967); and Rich, *The History of the Hudson's Bay Company, 1670–1870*, 2 vols. (London: Hudson's Bay Record Society, 1958–59). Invaluable to the student of the trade particularly as it affected Michilimackinac, Astor, and the Old Northwest is Paul C. Phillips, *The Fur Trade*, 2 vols. (Norman: University of Oklahoma Press, 1961). See also Wayne E. Stevens, *The Northwest Fur Trade 1763–1800* (Urbana: University of Illinois Press, 1926); and, for the later period, Theodore J. Karamanski, *Fur Trade and Exploration: Opening the Far Northwest, 1821–1852* (Norman: University of Oklahoma Press, 1983).

Exploration history is well served by the following authors: William H. Goetzmann, *New Lands, New Men: America and the Second Great Age of Discovery* (New York: Viking, 1986); John L. Allen, "To Unite the Discoveries: American Response to Early Exploration of Rupert's Land," in *Rupert's Land: A Cultural Tapestry*, ed. Richard C. Davis (Waterloo: Wilfrid Laurier University Press, 1988), pp. 79–96; and Carlos Schwantes, ed., *Encounters with a Distant Land: Exploration and the Great Northwest* (Moscow: University of Idaho Press, 1994). For a comprehensive northern reference, no better source exists than Clive Holland, *Arctic Exploration and Development, c. 500 B.C. to 1915: An Encyclopedia* (New York: Garland, 1994), which devotes attention to the role of the North West Company and various traders in northwestern exploration. On John Franklin's assessment of Mackenzie's scientific observations, the best source is Trevor H. Levere, *Science and the Canadian Arctic: A Century of Exploration, 1818–1918* (Cambridge: Cambridge University Press, 1993). See also Richard Davis, ed., *Sir John Franklin's Journals and Correspondence: The First Arctic Land Expedition, 1819–1822* (Toronto: Champlain Society, 1995). Mackenzie's advice to Lieutenant John Franklin in 1819 is in the Scott Polar Research Institute, Cambridge, England. Comments, possibly by Sir Joseph Banks or one of his associates, on Mackenzie's memorandum to Governor John Graves Simcoe in 1793 are to be found in the Banks Collection of the Sutro Library, San Francisco; they have been published by Richard H. Dillon, "An Alexander Mackenzie Letter, 1793," *British Columbia Historical Quarterly* 16 (July 1952): 209–10. Mrs. Simcoe's diary is found in an edition by J. Ross Robertson (1911; reprint, Toronto: Coles, 1973); it is also available in a better edition, Mary Quayle Innis, ed., *Mrs. Simcoe's Diary* (Toronto: Macmillan, 1965).

Numerous biographies exist of fur-trading contemporaries of Sir Alexander Mackenzie. Readers may wish to consult the following entries in *The Dictionary of Canadian Biography,* listed here in order of importance to Mackenzie: Barry Gough, "Pond, Peter," 5:681–86; Jean Morrison, "MacKay, Alexander," 5:532–34; Fernand Ouellet, "McGillivray, William" 6:454–57; Pierre Dufour, "Leroux, Laurent" 8:500–501; and J. I. Cooper, "Waddens [also Vuadens, Wadins], Jean-Etienne," 4:757. The following provide assistance in seeing the complexities of human relations during the period when Mackenzie flourished in the fur trade: Harold A. Innis, *Peter Pond: Fur Trader and Adventurer* (Toronto: Irwin and Gordon, 1930); Marjorie Wilkins Campbell, *McGillivray, Lord of the Northwest* (Toronto: Clarke Irwin, 1962; revised edition, *Northwest to the Sea: A Biography of William McGillivray,* Toronto: Clarke Irwin, 1975); James MacGregor, *Peter Fidler: Canada's Forgotten Surveyor 1769–1822* (Toronto: McClelland and Stewart, 1966); and John Denis Haeger, *John Jacob Astor: Business and Finance in the Early Republic* (Detroit: Wayne State University Press, 1991). See also James Ronda, *Astoria and Empire* (Lincoln: University of Nebraska Press, 1990). Travel anecdotes are to be found in John J. Bigsby, *The Shoe and Canoe, or Pictures of Travel in the Canadas,* 2 vols. (London, 1850; reprint, New York: Paladin, 1949).

Numerous histories of fur posts and fur trade areas exist, and the following recent works are of value: Patricia A. McCormack and R. Geoffrey Ironside, eds., *The Uncovered Past: Roots of Northern Alberta Societies*

(Edmonton: University of Alberta, 1993); Daniel Francis and Michael Payne, *A Narrative History of Fort Dunvegan* (Winnipeg: Watson and Dwyer, 1993). Related works include the following: Hugh MacLennan, *Rivers of Canada* (Toronto: Macmillan of Canada, 1974); Jennifer Brown, *Strangers in Blood: Fur Trade Company Families in Indian Country* (Vancouver: University of British Columbia Press, 1980; reprint, Norman: University of Oklahoma Press, 1996); and Sylvia Van Kirk, *Many Tender Ties: Women in Fur-Trade Society* (Winnipeg: Watson and Dwyer, 1980; reprint, Norman: University of Oklahoma Press, 1983).

The passages through the wilderness by Lewis and Clark can be traced through various editions of their journals, especially that published by the University of Nebraska Press (*The Journals of the Lewis and Clark Expedition*, ed. Gary E. Moulton, 5 vols. to date [1983–]). Criticism of Lewis by David McKeehan and related references to Mackenzie can be found in Donald Jackson, ed., *Letters of the Lewis and Clark Expedition with Related Documents, 1783–1854* (Urbana: University of Illinois Press, 1962).

The native history upon which any Mackenzie biography must rest is massive. Among other sources of specific value are William Sloan's biography of Aw-gee-nah, the English Chief (Mackenzie's Nestabeck), in *Dictionary of Canadian Biography*, 6:20. Sloan's biography may be supplemented by references in Harry Duckworth, ed., *The English River Book* (Montreal: McGill-Queen's University Press, 1989); and William Sloan, "Native Response to the Extension of the European Traders into the Athabasca and Mackenzie Basin, 1770–1814," *Canadian Historical Review* 60 (1979): 281–99. Mackenzie's Pacific journey has not received the same sort of detailed examination from historians as his 1789 voyage. In the naming and designating of native tribes, language groups, and bands, the work of John R. Swanton is still useful: *The Indian Tribes of North America* (Washington, D.C.: Smithsonian Institution, 1952). Of special value is *DEHCHO: "We've Been Discovered!"* (Yellowknife: Dene Cultural Institute, 1989). For lands west of the Continental Divide, worthwhile works include the following: *Ulkatcho Stories of the Grease Trail: Anahim Lake, Bella Coola, Quesnel*, told by Ulkatcho and Nuxalk elders, written by Sage Birchwater (Anahim Lake, B.C.: Ulkatcho Indian Band, 1993); T. F. McIlwaith, *The Bella Coola Indians*, 2 vols. (Toronto: University of Toronto Press, 1948); and Dorothy Kennedy and Randall Bouchard, "Bella Coola," in *Handbook of North American Indians, Volume 7: Northwest Coast*, ed. Wayne Suttles (Washington, D.C.: Smithsonian Institution,

1990). The "vertical file" on Sir Alexander Mackenzie in the British Columbia Provincial Archives and Records Service in Victoria, British columbia, contains treasures, including Jacobsen's interview and Mackenzie King's statement. Mackenzie found an aboriginal world suffering greatly from numerical losses because of diseases, as he pointed out in his book (1801 ed., pp. xiv–xv, liii, lxxvii–lxxviii, and lxxxii). Fur traders' and explorers' observations on smallpox and other diseases are today the subject of close scrutiny. Preliminary findings by Colebrook Harris indicate the arrival of smallpox on the British Columbia coast before British and Spanish discoveries. In interpreting fur trade documents and texts, I have used with profit Jennifer Brown, "Fur Trade History as Text and Drama," in *The Uncovered Past: Roots of Northern Alberta Societies* (Edmonton: University of Alberta, 1993); and Ian S. MacLaren, "Exploration/Travel Literature and the Evolution of the Author," *International Journal of Canadian Studies* 5 (Spring 1992): 39–68. Future voyageurs and travelers in search of Mackenzie should consult John Woodworth and Halle Flygare, *In the Steps of Alexander Mackenzie,* second edition (Box 425, Stn. A, Kelowna, B.C., V1Y 7P1: The Alexander Mackenzie Voyageur Route Association, 1989); Eric W. Morse, *Fur Trade Canoe Routes of Canada: Then and Now,* second edition (Toronto: University of Toronto Press, 1971); and, if going by air, the delightful work by Robert J. Hing, *Tracking Mackenzie to the Sea: Coast to Coast in Eighteen Splashdowns* (Manassas, Va.: Anchor Watch, 1992).

Index